I0816319

YOUR Highest Vibration

About the Author

Jiulio Consiglio (Ontario, Canada) is a spiritual teacher and author who focuses on the transformative power of inner stillness, the mind-body-spirit connection, and psychic abilities development. His message is that there is life beyond fear and incessant thinking, and it is found in the dimension of inner stillness. Jiulio is the author of *Open Your Third Eye* and *Your Inner Healer*, and a contributor to *Finding Your Calm* and offers consciousness-based teachings to individuals and groups. Visit him at www.JiulioConsiglio.com.

To Write to the Author

If you wish to contact the author or would like more information about this book, please write to the author in care of Llewellyn Worldwide Ltd. and we will forward your request. Both the author and the publisher appreciate hearing from you and learning of your enjoyment of this book and how it has helped you. Llewellyn Worldwide Ltd. cannot guarantee that every letter written to the author can be answered, but all will be forwarded. Please write to:

Jiulio Consiglio
℅ Llewellyn Worldwide
2143 Wooddale Drive
Woodbury, MN 55125-2989

Please enclose a self-addressed stamped envelope for reply, or $1.00 to cover costs. If outside the U.S.A., enclose an international postal reply coupon.

Many of Llewellyn's authors have websites with additional information and resources. For more information, please visit our website at https://www.llewellyn.com.

YOUR Highest Vibration

Realize Your Full Potential *through* CHAKRA WORK *and* MEDITATION

JIULIO CONSIGLIO

WOODBURY, MINNESOTA

First Edition
First Printing, 2026

Book design by Samantha Peterson
Cover design by Shannon McKuhen
Interior illustrations by Llewellyn Art Department

Library of Congress Cataloging-in-Publication Data (Pending)
ISBN: 978-0-7387-8012-2

Llewellyn Publications
A Division of Llewellyn Worldwide Ltd.
2143 Wooddale Drive
Woodbury, MN 55125-2989
www.llewellyn.com

Printed in the United States of America

GPSR Representation:
UPI-2M PLUS d.o.o., Medulićeva 20, 10000 Zagreb, Croatia,
matt.parsons@upi2mbooks.hr

Other Books by Jiulio Consiglio

Open Your Third Eye:
Activate Your Sixth Chakra &
Develop Your Psychic Abilities

Finding Your Calm:
Twelve Methods to Release Anxiety,
Relieve Stress & Restore Peace

Your Inner Healer:
Using Chakras and Energy
Medicine to Achieve Wholeness

This book is dedicated to all those who have been searching for the keys to unlocking their potential. May this book serve as a reminder that what you seek is already within you. Many blessings to you all as you remember the power of awareness in activating your untapped spiritual faculties that will guide and assist you in realizing your highest potential.

Contents

Meditations and Exercises

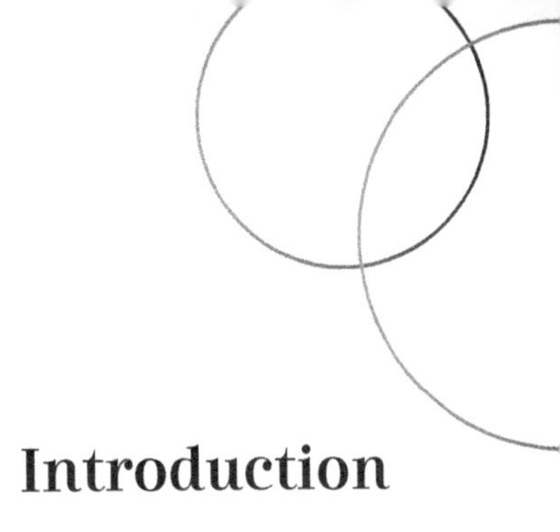

Introduction

You are the very portal, the doorway, to not only realizing your highest timeline but also embodying the highest version of yourself through clarity and expanded awareness. You, and you alone, are responsible for the way you feel, your outlook, what you believe, and the energy that you operate from, all of which make up your vibrational frequency. It's not your circumstances, your past, nor your current challenges that are standing in your way, but rather your perception of them. You are deciding the level of difficulty, and whether something is possible, based on either the limitations of the past or the potential of the now—the present moment.

Being expressions of consciousness, the chakras are teeming with energy, healing power, and timeline- or reality-shifting potential. But as transformative as they are, these incredible and life-changing energy wheels can become blocked, stagnant, and limited when left unattended through outer distraction, fear, and limiting beliefs. The good news is that when we understand the role they play in our state of being, emotions, energy levels, and ability to move forward and consciously manifest our lives, we can choose to work with them. This conscious partnership with the chakras shifts us from resistance to flow, healing, inner balance, and illumination.

My goal for this book is to reveal the chakras' potential through insights and coach you with transformative meditations and exercises as I assist you in facilitating your own inner healing and the rediscovery of your inner power and potential. It's my deepest desire, as we journey together through this process of remembering and reconnecting, to have you realize that your complete and fifth-dimensional, light-filled spiritual self is here and now, ever ready and available to guide, inspire, and empower you.

Harnessing Chakra Power

The main chakra system is a set of seven energy wheels that are located within the subtle body, along the spine, beginning at its base, and traveling upward toward the top of the head. The subtle or light body is unseen but can be felt as waves of energy when one is in tune with it through meditation. It connects the soul or spiritual realm with the physical body or manifested world. The chakras serve as sources for stability, playfulness, self-empowerment, compassion, expression, intuition, and spiritual connection. As we bring awareness and work in harmony with them, we can allow healing, renew our strength, and live a more peaceful, healthy, and empowered life.

Working with the chakra system has been an incredibly empowering experience, as I've been able to access their restorative potential, insights, intuition, and clarity. Being consciously aware and connected in mind, body, and spirit has allowed me to anchor into the present as I tune in to higher dimensions of consciousness. This awareness—of the chakras' abilities to guide—has provided me the direction to express my highest potential, as resistance has been released and replaced by inner flow, knowing, and these powerful forces: faith and trust. As our navigation system for every facet of our lives, the chakra system is an extension of the soul and its wisdom, which includes profound discernment.

This book will focus on chakra awareness and their application in your everyday life, what creates blocks in them and how to become aware when this happens, as well as how to connect, heal, and open them. Being aware of when we're feeling stuck energetically is a large part of the healing process—we can't heal that of which we're unaware. Awareness leads to insight and clarity, which leads to conscious action, allowing one to move forward. Knowing when an inner shift is required and when release is called for is key to being able to come into and maintain balance.

We're going to look at each chakra individually and use various meditations, intentions, and affirmations to consciously connect to, heal, activate, and work with them. As insights and clarity surrounding these powerful energetic wheels are offered, you will gain an understanding of their inner workings and potential to serve you in a positive way. This will give you the direction needed on how to work with them harmoniously, healing not only your inner world but also your outer world. As you shift into the next grandest version of yourself, so do the facets of your life—your relationships, health, ideas of abundance—and your timeline reflects that.

Being Disconnected Versus Connected to the Chakras

Each chakra, or energy wheel, pertains to a certain area in the physical body, as well as feelings and emotions, which then impact your state of being, positive or negative. The heart chakra, for example, is the fourth main chakra, located in the chest. It's associated with the heart, lungs, and circulatory system. On a spiritual and positive energetic level, this chakra is the center of unconditional love—for oneself and others—as well as compassion, kindness, joy, empathy, and forgiveness.

On the flip side, when we're disconnected from our heart space, the negative emotions that energetically block the heart chakra are hate, anger, and resentment, primarily. When we experience negative emotion toward another, anger for example, that projected energy is immediately returned to the heart center because on a spiritual level, we're all one. Reaction is a form of self-attack. In fact, this is an example of the hidden mechanics of how the chakras are affected by "external" forces: through the repeating of the outer in the inner. There really is no one, nothing, outside of you, because physical reality and everything in it is an extension of your consciousness—it's all you. Despite appearances of separateness, there ultimately is only oneness.

As we become aware of the chakras and their function within us, we come into greater clarity and self-understanding. We're dealing with energy here, and to balance out lower vibrational, negative energy, we need awareness and higher vibrational, positive energy, such as clarity and the forgiveness that extends from it. Keep in mind—and this is important to mention—forgiveness is not just about releasing the other person of their trespasses but more so about releasing ourselves of the burdens that come with holding on to anger. When we can see the immense value in forgiving, which unblocks and heals the heart chakra, we release ourselves of the past and the emotional pain associated with it. That's not to say those negative emotions won't creep up anymore, because they can. The difference, however, is that when we're connected to our heart chakra, for example, we are in tune with its wisdom, energy, and compassion, and so we respond instead of react.

Being heart-centered reminds us to let go rather than harbor and hold on. It's this conscious approach that starts the healing process; the dissolving of negativity as to allow the free-flowing and healing power of universal energy, channeled through the chakras, to do what it's intended to do: restore and maintain our inner balance.

Becoming Illuminated

Your inner being, the authentic self, contains the chakra system and is already whole, complete, and illuminated. The state of enlightenment, where every chakra is open, activated, and lit up, reflects your spiritual self—who you were, and still are, before human conditioning and ego identity. It's important to state that there's nothing wrong with the ego, nor is there anything wrong with experiencing negative emotion.

The ego is a part of our spiritual evolution, for you cannot know and appreciate who you really are until you experience that which you are not. The ego initially serves as our identity and forms a personality based on our experiences and environment. Issues arise when the ego, with its reactionary nature, goes unchecked, creating an imbalance of excess negative energy and the mental roadblocks to actualizing our full potential.

The ego is the contrast—you could say *the darkness*—to our inner light of consciousness, which is stillness. Stillness is unconditional love, transcendent of fear and attachments, and it's who you are at your core.

The ego also offers the perspectives (mind constructs) of past and future. From a spiritual vantage point, the ego ultimately serves the sole (soul) purpose of being the catalyst for awakening from the dreaming world of thought to the present and clear state of stillness and your illuminated self.

What I want to make clear is nothing must be added to you, but rather we are to look at what's no longer serving us, keeping us stuck, and preventing us from living an empowered, fulfilling life, in all its facets. Healing is a return to wholeness where mind, body, and spirit are operating in unison; experienced as inner peace, wisdom, clarity, intuition, and unconditional love. The chakras, when activated and lit up, raise your vibrational frequency, energy, and awareness, making it possible for you to embody your inner light that unleashes extraordinary potential.

Your Highest Timeline

Being consciously connected to the highest self through inner stillness activates extraordinary potentials and shifts you into your highest timeline. Your highest timeline represents inner and outer fulfillment (the unfolding of your desires) through activated potentials. By operating through inner knowing, through surrender, and by taking action through divine guidance, you invite desirable experiences and an optimal life consciously. This state of being—an experience beyond inner conflict and resistance—allows for the highest self to express itself through you as an expanded and fearless version of you. This is not to say that there won't be challenges, but through clarity and intuition, you will be able to navigate life more confidently with a spirit of fearlessness. When you are centered in unconditional love and compassion, you extend these spiritual attributes only to receive them again and again because all of life is a mirror.

You don't create your highest timeline but rather align with it by making the inner shift beyond ego, beyond the thinking mind, and into the dimension of inner stillness—the state of "no mind." This elevated vibrational frequency is a state of being that is free of thought but teeming with divine intelligence, potential, and possibility. Because it is the mind of Source, stillness is unbound, unlimited, and the birthplace of miracles, where all things are possible. Reflecting your highest vibration, being fully conscious of inner stillness unlocks your full potential.

As we journey together, you'll be given the opportunity to do the inner work and face your shadows so you can transmute them through the power of your awareness. I often say, "awareness is everything" because through centered present-moment awareness we align with Source and the healing power of universal energy that is unconditional love and transformative by nature. You don't have to try but rather apply, not resist or fight against the darkness but look at it with fearlessness.

I also want to remind you that your highest timeline is already a potential within you. Aligning with it starts with the process of letting go—of who you thought you were and the limiting beliefs that come with ego identification. While embodying stillness, the ego dissolves along with its struggles to reveal pure consciousness: the highest self. Spiritual awakening and the healing that follows is a process of subtraction, of releasing all that you're not so you can remember and be all that you are in spirit.

What Led Me to My Highest Timeline

Between the ages of nineteen and thirty-three, I experienced tremendous personal challenges that came in the form of years of intense anxiety and the depression that came with it. Experiencing the negative emotions that bombarded me daily led to not only personal suffering but also difficulty in navigating life. Further compounding the negativity that I struggled with for several years, in the winter of 2004, at the age of thirty-two, I was given a cancer diagnosis. On the surface, it appeared that my life was headed for disaster. Little did I know what all that suffering was preparing me for. It was creating the perfect conditions for a spontaneous third eye awakening and the remembrance of who I am beyond the thinking mind.

In the fall of 2005, after experiencing what I have described as a "lifetime of pain," I made a shift in awareness. I made a quantum leap from ego consciousness to the dimension of inner stillness or third-dimensional (3D) to fifth-dimensional (5D) consciousness in the "twinkling of an eye." Stillness is a state of being beyond thought; it is the unified field—the spiritual realm—and all the potential found within it. The potential I'm talking about is every possible experience or reality, desired or undesired. Through the clarity of stillness, I have allowed spontaneous healing on every level. Insights, wisdom, and the understanding of spirit remind me of who and where I am. I have remembered that I am a spiritual being first, and with that inner realization, I have been able to see past the manifested world around me and recognize consciousness flowing through everything and everyone.

In knowing who I am, and what is possible, I have chosen to focus and align with that which reflects who I've become. I'm no longer swayed nor moved by what I see out there, which includes circumstances. I instead choose consciously how I want to feel by embodying it. It's by tending to my vibrational frequency—choosing peace, happiness, joy, and abundance as states of being—that I have shifted into the unlimited potentials of stillness or consciousness. I've realized that to experience anything, one must first become it vibrationally.

The Purpose of This Book

This book was brought to life as humanity is going through a collective shift in consciousness from ego and separation consciousness to soul awareness and unity consciousness. Personal transformation is often turbulent and confusing, leaving us with many questions. Knowing this, I felt it crucial to offer a guide at this time that provides deep insights into our spiritual and energetic selves. In revealing the root causes for our personal adversities and suffering, and by offering my experience, strategies, and messages from higher dimensions, my desire is to assist you on your healing journey as you are reminded of your personal power.

If you feel comfortable enough, you can apply the exercises and meditations as you encounter them during reading. If you are new to the chakras and spirituality, it would probably be best to approach this book by first reading it in its entirety, as to grasp the spiritual concepts offered, and then go back and start the activities with a more grounded approach. My intention is for you to get the most out of this guide, and I suggest you refer to it often. I have found that missed insights are often revealed later, when we are ready to receive them.

Wishing you an extraordinary journey toward realizing your highest vibration and potential. A thousand blessings.

ONE
Chakras 101: *Overview and Potential*

There are seven main chakras, or energy wheels, within the subtle body, or light body. The chakras, when open and activated, illuminate you from within, clear your energy field, and usher in healing, inner balance, and a deep sense of well-being. This in turn offers clarity and allows you to tune in to your spiritual nature and operate from a mind, body, and soul awareness (spiritual embodiment). From this elevated level of awareness, you can tap into your potential, get unstuck, and make massive shifts forward in your life. By activating and working with these reality-shifting portals of power, you shift into the next grandest version of yourself, as you unlock your spiritual faculties and the tools necessary to live a fulfilling and successful life.

The chakras harness universal, or cosmic, energy and maintain that energy, or *prana*, within the physical body. These energy centers, or points of power, move in a clockwise fashion when they function unimpeded. In a centered and energetically balanced state, you are impacting the outer world with your light and state of being, as the chakras spin high-frequency universal

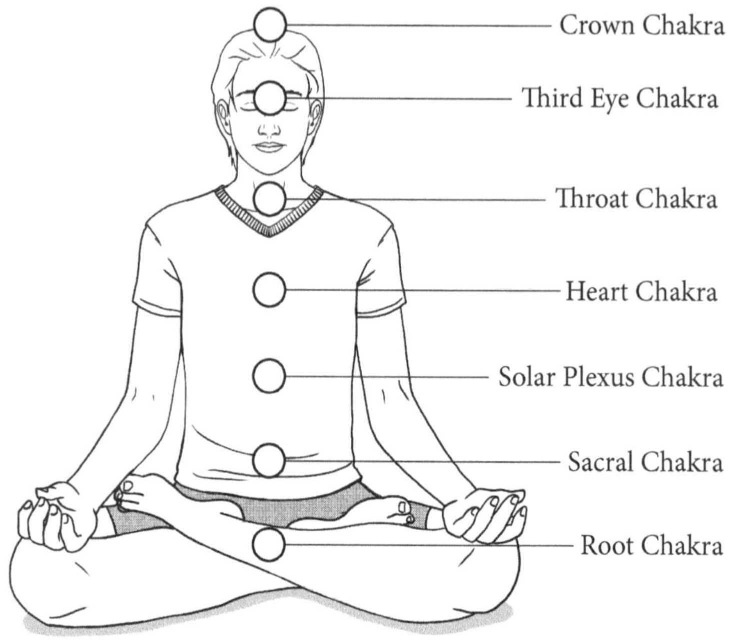

energy out of the physical body. Conversely, when there's some level of energetic imbalance, the chakras are blocked or moving counterclockwise because there is accumulated negative emotion. In this impressionable state, the chakras will pull in contracted energy that causes one to be impacted by seeming external forces. This leads to feeling stuck in life, which is a result of feeling stuck energetically.

The subtle body connects the soul to the physical body. It is the bridge between your spiritual nature (your unmanifested self) and your physical body. Not entirely spiritual or physical, it is an in-between energy body that connects the spiritual realm and the manifested world. The subtle body can be experienced as waves of energy in and around your body through deep awareness and meditation. The subtle body is an extension of the soul, and as such it is the intelligence responsible for all of your body's functions, including healing. It has great potential that comes in the form of the chakras. When tuned in to and allowed to guide us, it can express itself through us as extraordinary health and vitality.

My goal is to give you a clear picture of the different parts that make up *you*. We're going to look at mind, body, and soul so you can cultivate greater discernment as to when you're experiencing ego versus the soul. The first state is fearful and contracting in nature, while the soul is fearless, inspiring, and expansive.

Our Mind, Body, and Spiritual Makeup

I've listed our various aspects here, for reference, further clarity, and self-understanding. Being foundational for personal growth, self-understanding provides the discernment needed to not only understand how one operates but also know and recognize when fear presents itself and to approach it consciously.

Conscious Mind: Also called local mind. This is your individual mind, which is positive in nature, that's aware and focused on your local surroundings, or the here and now. Your conscious mind reflects the higher mind or the mind of Source and is silent in nature.

Ego: The automatic thinker and personal identity that one takes on as a human being. Operates between the past and the future. The ego is fear itself and is the source for all negative emotion and our suffering.

Nonlocal Mind: This is the universal mind of Source, which you're always connected to. It is unbound and unlimited in nature and reflects stillness; no-thing in particular. It can also be described as the unified field, as it's all-encompassing.

Physical Body: The physical vessel that simultaneously contains and is contained within the soul. Being mostly made of space, the body is essentially a holographic manifestation that is connected to the mind and soul.

Soul: This is your inner being, or authentic self, and it is unconditional love. It is an extension of Source and emanates stillness: silence. The soul is clarity, wisdom, and understanding, and in embodying the soul, you bring these attributes to life. The soul is accessed through the present moment or now.

Subtle Body: That which connects the soul to the physical body. It is divine intelligence that is responsible for your body's functions and healing. It also houses your inner guidance system in the form of the chakras.

We're now going to look at the individual aspects that make up your experience of being human—mind, body, and soul.

The Mind

Your conscious mind, or local mind, is an individuation of the boundless higher mind. This point of awareness perceives the here and now. Your mind and soul, although multidimensional, give you the individual experience of your current whereabouts and translate that through your senses.

The Body

Your physical body is what takes all that you are on a spiritual and energetic level and translates that through your senses. It reflects our inner world. It can reflect health or sickness, strength or weakness, youthfulness or aging based on one's vibrational frequency. We are the energy, thoughts, words, and emotions we align and identify with, which is good news. Because if we're dealing with energy, then we can take greater self-responsibility and do the inner work—releasing and forgiving—to change our field of energy and renew ourselves in mind, body, and soul.

The Soul

Your soul is always connected and one with everything and everyone, including Source. It is eternal, indestructible, and invulnerable. The soul is the source for your inspiration. It is spontaneous by nature, and when you're consciously aligned with it, you're able to be inspired and guided, allowing you to tap into creativity. The soul reflects stillness, which means that when you're deeply aware and aligned with the present moment and one with spirit, that translates to a quiet mind.

The Powerful Individual Mind

Your individual or local mind is what calls forth your experiences, and ultimately, your reality, through belief. This is done on either an unconscious or a conscious level, depending on whether one identifies and is in alignment with the ego (thinking mind) or the soul (stillness). Your experience is based on the quality of your inner world of thoughts, emotions, words, and outlook, all of which make up your inner energetic field (vibrational frequency) in which you align with or repel your desires.

Always connected to the higher mind, the mind of Source, your individual mind is powerful and requires discernment, focus, and direction. The baseline for your local mind is also silent, as it reflects the higher mind and is free of thought. Like the soul, your still, silent mind is encountered in the present moment through awareness. It's important to distinguish your true, real mind relative to the ever-changing and illusory nature of the egoic mind, which we'll look at next.

The Ego

It is important to introduce the ego, or thinking mind, as well. It is an essential concept because it is a huge part of shadow work—bringing light to the darkness. The ego or shadow self is first and foremost a necessary part of your personal evolution. From a spiritual perspective, the ego is neither good nor bad; it simply is what it is. It gives us a sense of personal identity while also giving us a sense of being separate from each other and life itself. The ego is fear disguised as various negative emotions. It is the moving energy of thought forms relative to our still, spiritual self.

The ego operates and perpetuates itself through the past and the future. It's our belief in these mind constructs and our identifying with them that make them seem so real. But here's the thing: if you were to reflect on the concepts of past/future and really examine them, you would realize that the past is only experienced in our minds as memories (good and bad) and emotions such as regret, sadness, guilt, and past-based happiness. There's nothing wrong with that.

With regard to the future, it never arrives. It is experienced through projection and anticipation, even excitement, but it is often experienced as worry, anxiety, uncertainty, and even doubt. All of this is necessary for our human experience and is responsible for the accumulated layers of emotion that not only hijack our consciousness, but also, if I'm going to be blunt, impact and block our chakra system, depending on the emotion.

Chakra System

We're going to look at the chakra system and briefly look at each individual chakra to create a foundation. Perspective is important here as we dive into the world of spirit and energy. It's important to remember that we have physical bodies, but we are not our bodies; we are eternal, spiritual beings having a temporary human experience. This perspective will allow the information to resonate further, permitting greater clarity and understanding. With this awareness, making inner, positive shifts is easier.

The chakra system is pure potential, as it's an extension of the soul. There is nothing that the soul cannot accomplish because it is boundless and transcendent of the limitations of this world. To unlock the potential of this powerful energy system, awareness needs to be introduced. It's awareness that takes dormant forces and activates them, unleashing their potential. The chakra system makes up the subtle body, connecting universal or cosmic energy to the physical body.

Looking at these energy wheels more closely, we begin with the root chakra and move upward:

Root Chakra

Description and Responsible For: The foundation of the chakra system, it provides inner stability and security.

Location: Base of spine—closest to the earth

Associated Organs/Body Area: Adrenal glands, colon, bones, and pelvic region

Emotional Balance: Feeling grounded, self-responsibility, stability

Symptoms of Blocked Energy: Worry, fear, fatigue

Color and Element Associated: Red, as it represents our entry into the manifested world; earth; rooted

Affirmations for Balance: "I am grounded and present." "I am safe and secure."

Positive and Healing Effects: Being grounded in your root chakra through present-moment awareness shifts you into a more empowered version of yourself. Being closer to spirit, you're able to observe fear rather than react to it, enabling you to navigate life with greater confidence. Anchored in the now is what invites clarity and the discernment to see fear for what it is: illusory. Giving us the ability to release fears through greater spiritual alignment, a balanced root chakra opens us up to possibility and the abundance that life has to offer.

Sacral Chakra

Description and Responsible For: Allows for the expression of playfulness, sensuality, and seeing the lighter side of life.

Location: Below the navel

Associated Organs/Body Area: Reproductive organs, womb, bladder, and kidneys

Emotional Balance: Lightheartedness, feeling attractive, healthy boundaries

Symptoms of Blocked Energy: Fear of intimacy, lack of creativity, emotional instability

Color and Element Associated: Orange, as it represents joy and purity; water; flow

Affirmations for Balance: "I am fun and playful." "I am attractive and magnetic."

Positive and Healing Effects: Being connected to the sacral chakra allows you to not take life too seriously, as you become more lighthearted. Emotions move freely through you, as you're able to see them as being part of your inner guidance system, not who you are. An activated and open sacral chakra brings us into greater harmony with ourselves and our relationships, making for the cultivation of happier and healthier relationships.

Solar Plexus Chakra

Description and Responsible For: Personal power, willpower, and boundaries

Location: Upper abdomen area

Associated Organs/Body Area: Digestive system, liver, spleen, and gallbladder

Emotional Balance: Clear sense of purpose, self-confidence, decisive

Symptoms of Blocked Energy: Being needy, poor self-esteem; having a victim mentality

Color and Element Associated: Yellow, as it represents energy; fire; rebirth

Affirmations for Balance: "I am confident and powerful." "I am worthy of happiness and success."

Positive and Healing Effects: Resonating with the solar plexus chakra connects us with our personal power. Realizing the energy-shifting power of your will, you know you can consciously change your inner state, thereby shaping your reality. Understanding that you are always supported and guided, you're equipped to face challenges with greater confidence. A free-flowing solar plexus chakra is what shifts one from living from the outside-in (reactive to the outer world) to the inside-out (where one now impacts their environment).

Heart Chakra

Description and Responsible For: Center for unconditional love, forgiveness, and compassion

Location: Center of the chest

Associated Organs/Body Area: Heart, lungs, circulatory system, arms, and hands

Emotional Balance: Ability to forgive, love unconditionally, experience inner happiness

Symptoms of Blocked Energy: Harboring anger and resentment; not willing to forgive and let go

Color and Element Associated: Green, as it represents charitable love; air; compassion

Affirmations for Balance: "I am unconditional love." "I extend love and am worthy of love."

Positive and Healing Effects: Being heart-centered creates balance and harmony between your lower and upper chakras. In becoming more harmonious with yourself and others, an activated heart chakra brings forth your true, authentic spiritual self. Mindful of the releasing power of forgiveness and compassion, you are free to move past and heal from emotional issues experienced in relationships. In this elevated state of being, you're not afraid to give or receive love.

Throat Chakra

Description and Responsible For: The ability to express yourself and higher truths

Location: Center of throat

Associated Organs/Body Area: Mouth, tongue, pharynx, and neck

Emotional Balance: Confident to express oneself, honoring your spiritual truths, authentic communication

Symptoms of Blocked Energy: Fearful to express oneself, feeling unheard; timid

Color and Element Associated: Blue, as it represents calm communication; ether; space

Affirmations for Balance: "I am able to express myself authentically." "I am a great listener and communicator."

Positive and Healing Effects: A balanced throat chakra allows for authentic and honest communication. Especially beneficial to relationships, being able to express oneself as a matter arises not only offers clarity but also allows for easier navigation through the usual relationship emotions that tend to arise such as anger and resentment because of misunderstanding. Effective communication, which includes active listening, is key to experiencing greater harmony in our day-to-day interactions.

Third Eye Chakra

Description and Responsible For: Enlightenment; clarity, wisdom, intuition, and understanding

Location: Forehead area, between and just above the eyebrows

Associated Organs/Body Area: Pineal gland

Emotional Balance: Fearlessness, centered, self-awareness

Symptoms of Blocked Energy: Anxiety, depression; confusion

Color and Element Associated: Indigo, as it represents intuition; light; seeing

Affirmations for Balance: "I am clarity and wisdom." "I am intuitive and divinely guided."

Positive and Healing Effects: Operating through an activated and open third eye unlocks your highest potential. Challenges are met with greater confidence, and solutions are allowed to be expressed more rapidly due to clarity and nonresistance. A surrendered state of being allows the highest self to not only inspire but also to be expressed through the person's vibrational frequency, which is based in unconditional love. Knowing who you are relative to Source, you have a clear vision for your life, taking inner and outer action, as you let go of how and when it will manifest.

Crown Chakra

Description and Responsible For: Spiritual connection and the experience of oneness

Location: Top of head

Associated Organs/Body Area: Brain, the pituitary gland, and the pineal gland

Emotional Balance: Clear-minded, spiritually connected, inner peace

Symptoms of Blocked Energy: Materially focused, disconnected, lacking purpose

Color and Element Associated: Purple, as it represents spirituality; not associated with physical elements (transcendent)

Affirmations for Balance: "I am one with Source." "I am a limitless spiritual being."

Positive and Healing Effects: An open crown chakra immerses you into the vastness, potential, and universal energy of Spirit. A shift into universal or cosmic consciousness helps one realize their interconnectedness with all of life. Transcendent of the limitations of the thinking mind, one begins to think, imagine, and speak through their spiritual self: the soul. The direct experience of Source, inner peace is experienced moment by moment as inner stillness. The thinking mind no longer dictates your state of being. You are now free to call forth the desired feeling instantly through intention. In this state, all things become possible, and desires are allowed to manifest with greater ease because there is no more doubt or inner conflict.

How the Chakras Work

You can look at every chakra as a faucet that controls the flow of universal energy—the water of life. The more closed off one is to their spiritual self, the more closed off they are to the restorative healing and potential of universal energy. As one grows and expands in spiritual awareness, the more shedding of limiting beliefs is allowed to take place. With that, greater light, as in light information, is allowed to return to one's awareness. With more light comes greater discernment, clarity, insight, enhanced psychic abilities, and understanding. Since our minds regulate the flow of light and universal energy, our awareness (or lack thereof) is responsible for the opening/closing of the chakras.

I've come to realize just how vital and life-changing awareness is. Awareness shifts potential to possibility; it's what makes a dream become possible. Awareness, in a mindful sense, is what gives us the discernment to recognize darkness and face it so it can be transmuted. Being aware of how we've been operating and mindful of our self-sabotaging patterns is how we begin the process of releasing, moving forward, and expanding in consciousness.

The chakras respond to our inner state of being, whether we're in the dreaming state of thought or the awakened state of inner stillness. For example, when we're angry, the chakras contract, and when we're happy and going with the flow, they expand and spin freely. A part of consciousness itself, the chakra system is listening to you, waiting for your commands—positive or negative. Understanding this, we are empowered to cultivate greater self-awareness and discernment, moving forward.

Because the chakras respond to your inner world of thought, emotion, and outlook (your vibrational frequency), I want to offer five reminders to assist you in raising it, which in turn positively affects the chakra system. These are simple, yet powerful reminders that you can refer to as needed to help raise and maintain your energy.

Five Ways to Raise Your Vibrational Frequency

- Remember the present moment. The now is one of the keys to raising your vibrational frequency. Becoming aware of the moment and being mindful of it throughout the day not only centers us but also shifts our energy out of the lower energies of the past/future.
- Start becoming an observer to negative thought and emotion, rather than a reactor. This takes practice, but the more you bring awareness—presence—to the thinking mind, the greater clarity you will invite and, with that, a raising of your energetic field. Remember that by observing thought/emotion, you're not suppressing anything but introducing awareness. It's by the continuous practice of reacting that we accumulate more layers of emotion and pain.
- Circumstances don't matter. Everything is experienced in our mind, including circumstances. We can view them as positive, negative, and even neutral. Our outlook, what we see "out there," is reflected within us. Deciding to just be neutrally aware of and not give a negative connotation to a circumstance is self-empowering and uplifting, which raises our energy.

- Choose peace. This is an inside job. Being mindful of just how powerful we are as spiritual beings and how our inner world manifests our outer, we can choose not to give our vital energy away to fear and worry. We can choose peace and embody it by remembering that fear is not real but a construct of the thinking mind.
- Choose your thoughts consciously. We don't have to wait for outer change to experience inner happiness. We can experience it right now by choosing, becoming, and thinking or saying out loud, "I am happy. I am happiness." The effects from such positive affirmations are felt even deeper when expressed with knowing; with the awareness that what you're choosing now is made manifest as a feeling.

A large part in consciously working with the chakras is the concept of self-responsibility. By becoming aware that we can make positive inner shifts, despite what is going on around us, we become a more empowered version of ourselves. And with that, we can ascend in consciousness—toward the upper chakras, move forward, realizing possibilities as we grow, and expand in awareness—in consciousness. As you bring awareness to the chakras and bring them online by working with them, the result is enhanced clarity, intuition, and divine guidance that shifts you into more empowered states.

The Unified Field: Definition and Potentials

The *unified field* is a term used to describe the spiritual, unseen realm that encompasses our reality. It's the space all around us and within us, as it is the mind of Source. Within the field is every possibility and parallel reality one can imagine and beyond. Which reality or experience is called forth depends on who and what you're being in the moment. Life, what you experience "out there," is mirrored based on your vibrational frequency. For example, a negative mindset will see negativity; it will see the worst in everything and everyone. In contrast, a positive and uplifted mindset operates through gratitude, seeing the best in everyone and everything—even the perfection in it all—despite conditions.

You can look at life like a video game, in a sense. Every outcome is already preloaded. What you encounter or experience depends on your choosing—what direction you take. The good news is that if you've headed down a path that's been negative, challenging, and undesirable, you can change course and choose differently by doing the inner work, such as releasing the things that are no longer serving you, including limiting beliefs and negative emotions.

Within the unified field is also every potential version of you. That includes a version of you succeeding and experiencing all kinds of abundance. There's a version of you that's already enlightened with every chakra activated and open. There's a version of you already experiencing peace of mind. There's a version of you already experiencing extraordinary health and vitality. There's a version of you already making massive, positive changes in the world. And there's a version of you experiencing harmony in all your relationships. Every version of you—positive and negative—is a potential dependent on your vibrational frequency. This is but a glimpse of what's possible and waiting to be actualized in the unified field, for it houses infinite parallel realities based on our endless choices.

We're always shifting through countless versions of ourselves throughout the day through thoughts and emotions that are reflected in the world around us. Incredibly subtle, these inner and outer shifts become more obvious the closer one is to their spiritual nature and the stillness afforded through awareness. Every thought is a doorway to another experience or reality and those thoughts and subsequent emotions are based on one's level of awareness, powered by the chakra system. Before we go more into the concept of parallel realities, let's briefly look at the unified field where potential and possibility—including parallel realties—wait to be actualized.

There is a lot more going on in the unseen spiritual realm that surrounds us than one can imagine. Physical reality is but a grain of sand relative to the vastness of countless realities available to us. This is not to diminish the material world we live in and experience, but to give you an understanding that we are operating in a more fluid and multilayered reality, one that is not so concrete, despite appearances.

What we are describing here are energy and frequency. Physical reality is really energy that has coalesced into matter. Life and Source are one and the same. Within Source is potential and every possible experience that represents a particular frequency. Frequency refers to one's state of being (vibrational frequency), which stands for a particular experience on the surface or outlook. Nothing is set in stone; change is the isness of life—you can change your destiny and go beyond your current station in life, realize your highest potential and all it reflects through self-actualization.

Your imagination is key in homing in on that which you desire to experience or realize. It's powered by the third eye, or sixth chakra. The third eye is a powerful spiritual faculty that not only is the source of one's intuition but is also a powerful portal that aligns you with your desire through imagination. Acting like a doorway, it transports you to an energetic representation of the desire you want to see fulfilled in your mind. It is an opening to a potential, parallel reality. The power afforded to the third eye is extended through Source, as there is no separation; you and Source are one.

What you desire and imagine for your life is what Source desires and imagines for you. As you cultivate greater spiritual awareness and realize just what is possible, you will allow potentials (inspiration) to come to the forefront of your consciousness. This, in turn, will spark the desires as the first step in the allowing, or manifesting, process. Be mindful, you're not creating anything; creation is already complete, it's done. Everything that could possibly exist, does so, energetically, in the unified field—waiting to be brought to life—your life. What you're doing is deciding, aligning with, and resonating with the version of you already experiencing the fulfilled desire, through inner and outer action.

Insights into Source

Given that we're always working with Source Energy, I felt it important to provide a deeper look at Source for the purpose of greater understanding. From the awareness of inner stillness, clarity provides the following regarding Source: Source is everything because everything is within Source. It is unlimited and infinite intelligence—all knowing. There is nothing that Source is not. We are experiencing the one same energy, the One Life Force that experiences and expresses itself in countless ways. Source becomes what Source creates. Part of the awakening process is realizing that separation is an illusion—that you and Source are one. You and everything else and everyone else are one. This is why you can't project anger toward someone or something without immediately experiencing it within yourself. Conversely, it's why you can't extend kindness and compassion to another without immediately feeling it—becoming it first.

The experience of being one with Source is directly experienced through the dimension of inner stillness: a quiet mind. It's through stillness that thoughts of separation dissolve and the truth of your inner being (oneness) is revealed. Knowing and experiencing who and what you are spiritually is what reveals to you where you really are: the spiritual realm. Heaven on earth is a state of mind, often described as new earth—it's your spiritual awareness reflected outward. Physical reality is not so much material as it is energy, Source Energy.

Being omnipresent—which includes all space and time—Source knows ahead of time what you will choose for yourself. Source already knows where you'll hit some snags along your journey, and Source knows what your "future" reactions or responses will be. That's why the now is known as the present or "pre-sent." The importance of knowing and understanding this is that you can decide to make more life-affirming choices starting now, such as cultivating happiness and gratitude, which will invite more of the same in "future" moments. We're working with positive and negative energies, and what we focus on expands in the way we feel and experience life.

The importance of knowing who and where you are cannot be stated enough. Because all experience begins and ends within your mind—with you. Having an understanding and awareness of your spiritual reality, both inner and outer, shifts you toward higher timelines where you are not only embodying your spiritual nature but also experiencing the oneness of life, where true success abides. This leads us now to having a look at our highest potential from within.

Highest Potential Overview

When the chakras are healed, open, and functioning optimally, through self-awareness, nonattachment, and being in alignment with your highest self, that state of being will sooner or later be expressed as your highest potential within and without. My goal for this section is to paint a picture of how one's highest potential is experienced: first from within. Because the truth of the matter is that it all begins inside of you first—on an energetic level—at the level of mind, body, and soul. What I'll be describing is the enlightened state—the fifth dimensional version of you that is very much a potential and possibility, in this lifetime.

Your highest potential and its activation begins with the awareness of inner stillness. A quieted mind, being in alignment with stillness, raises your vibrational frequency beyond the thinking mind and into a state of quiet peace. It's a switch from the comings and goings of the thinking mind into the centeredness of your inner being. From this centered state, you're still able to experience thought and emotion but you're no longer attached to them—you're now free. In remembering your true spiritual identity through the silent witness that is the soul, you remember who you are in Source. It's by remembering your spiritual self that you understand your intrinsic worth and divine potential.

With your awareness anchored in the now, you are provided the clarity and strength to transmute fear and negativity as it arises because of the high-vibrating energy you're now operating from. You're no longer swayed by negative emotion or limiting beliefs. Negative thoughts or emotions no longer take days, weeks, or months to get over but are transmuted instantly in the presence of your inner being—unconditional love.

With the rediscovery of your spiritual essence, you begin to consciously select the feelings you wish to have. Having been healed of the perceived separation between yourself and Source, you also experience healing energetically through the power of unconditional love as it extends from your inner being toward the mind and body.

As a mind is healed, it will soon reconnect with its source and make direct contact with the soul—the authentic self, which will sooner or later translate into physical healing—the return to wholeness. The keys to coming back home, to reuniting consciously with the highest self, are desire and the spirit of surrender. Desire is the spark, that which sets off universal forces on your behalf to set the intention into motion. Surrender releases the resistance and inner conflict, which allows the highest self to express through you, as awakening, healing, and ultimately, your highest potential.

By embodying the highest self through awareness and the surrendered state, you are beyond the limitations of the egoic or conditioned mind. Through this state of being you transcend the concept of linear time, realizing the only moment there ever is: the eternal now. Desires at this level of awareness are allowed to manifest without much delay, as resistance and doubt have been laid aside. Operating through nonattachment, you let go of how and when the desire will manifest. You understand that desire is not the source of suffering, but rather the attachment to outcomes, and so you let go and let Source. Taking inspired action, when necessary, you assist in the merging of your fifth-dimensional potential/desire, to your third-dimensional manifested world.

Everyone's highest outer potential appears different, and that's very much okay. We are, of course, in a world of relativity, and everyone has their own desires and preferences. For some, it may be living a quiet life on a farm, working with the land. For others, it might be traveling the world, embracing adventure. For some, it may be to share their developed gifts and talents through art or singing. Discovering your life's purpose will most likely mean being of service in one form or another. Regardless of what kind of dream one is choosing to live, the key to expressing it begins within, with knowing the authentic self. Once free from self-created limitations, you enter the realm of spirit, where all things become possible, and you directly experience the source of all being. This unfolds through the presence of unconditional love as stillness and a peace that is beyond words.

Thinking and Speaking from Higher Awareness

Having offered an overview of how being one with the highest self reflects one's highest potential, I felt it vital to offer insights as to how the highest self thinks and speaks with regard to calling forth desired experiences and realities. These thoughts and words are not only raise vibrational frequency but also remind you of who you are spiritually, while simultaneously shifting you into desirable and uplifting frequencies. Remember that these thoughts and words are best expressed when you're clear on your spiritual identity—when you know who you are in Source. Having belief behind these affirmations is powerful, but coming from a space of knowing is even more so—knowing that what you think and speak is done.

The following twelve affirmations are representative of 5D awareness of being one with the highest self. They can be thought or spoken once or twice per day or as needed when you feel inspired. As you express these affirmations, come from the awareness that what you desire for your life is provided by Source.

Twelve Affirmations from Higher Awareness

- I am one with Source. Affirms your oneness
- What I desire for my life is what Source desires for me. Affirms and aligns your will with Source
- I am clarity, wisdom, and understanding. Affirms inner higher intelligence
- All that I desire shall come to fruition. Affirms all things are possible
- I am unlimited, as no limits have been laid upon me. Affirms the potential within you
- I am unconditional love and the peace that emanates from it. Affirms your inner being
- I am whole and complete now and always. Affirms nothing must be added to you
- I am already embodying the highest self and the potentials reflecting that. Affirms your spirituality
- I am living my highest potential now. Affirms your intention and focus
- I am living my life purpose and honoring it. Affirms your soul purpose
- Abundance and prosperity continuously flow through me and to me. Affirms your power to attract and align
- I am the embodiment of supernatural health, strength, and vitality. Affirms extraordinary health

Your highest potential is reflected by embodying the highest self and thinking, speaking, and acting upon that higher awareness.

TWO
Roadblocks and How to Get Unstuck

My goal in this chapter is to provide insight as to why we experience roadblocks, feel stuck at times, and haven't yet shifted into more desirable states of being and untapped potentials. With each adversity I shed light on, a solution will be offered. By highlighting these main reasons, we introduce awareness into the equation, which allows clarity to be invited, one of the keys to moving upward in consciousness and forward in life. At the core of any self-created roadblock is the ego, or thinking mind. Although the ego is our starting point of consciousness as human beings and who we think we are, it does not have to define us solely. There is a state of awareness beyond it, and it's already a potential within you. It's reflected through the high vibrational frequency emanating from one's inner being: the key to unleashing extraordinary potential.

The ego is a program, an artificial intelligence, relative to the infinite intelligence of Source. It's designed to focus on what has been and what could be, which contracts and limits our energy. It does this to keep one distracted from realizing the eternal moment of *now*—where self-actualization and personal freedom are available. When we exclusively identify with the ego and its limiting outlook and beliefs, we limit our potential and cut ourselves off from the expansiveness of universal energy. This energy is always flowing to us and through us, and the degree to which we receive it is based on our state of being. The conditioned mind is also responsible for the feeling of being separate from our highest self and the world around us.

Disguising itself as memories and projections, the ego has convinced us of its reality. But if you take a moment to reflect, you will realize that the past always arrived in the present, and that the future is but a thought that will only arrive in the now moment. What I'm alluding to is that the ego is the dreaming state of separation that walls us off from our inner being and the unimaginable potential it reflects.

The challenges or roadblocks we encounter are based in our perception of them and are in fact experienced in our minds. Essentially, there are two ways to look at a roadblock or a circumstance: as something that is keeping us stuck or as an opportunity to grow and shift past it through understanding. It's our outlook—positive or negative—and the kind of energy we pour into a perceived obstacle through belief and focus that makes it appear manageable or daunting.

Let's now look closer at some common self-created roadblocks and ways to not only overcome them but also grow in awareness in the process. In my own personal evolution process, I have realized that within every adversity was a gift waiting to be found; things like inner strength, clarity, determination, and the power of will, just to name a few. Because the truth of the matter is that challenges are not meant to keep us stuck but are to propel us forward. The conscious approach is to see them for what they are and learn the lesson that enables us to let them go and move toward higher vibrations and the highest self.

Fear and Ego

The ego is the source of fear because of what it is: a thought system that seemingly opposes not only your will for a fulfilling life but the will of the highest self as well. Because it's cut off from the light and unconditional love of consciousness—of stillness—it appears as the darkness. Being outwardly focused by nature, the ego branches off into many different forms of fear, depending on where it's being projected. Just as a tree has branches and bears its own fruit, so too does the ego branch off, making more of itself (fear) as it's fed with our vital energy and attention. Because of projection, many of us experience the fear of the unknown or the fear of public speaking. Many of us have also experienced the fear of being alone at one time or another. For some people, there's the fear of being in crowds. There's even the fear of success, referred to as "success anxiety" or "success phobia" and so on. But here's the thing; it's not the actual "thing" one is afraid of but the fear itself—the negative feelings at the thought of doing something, and potential feelings that can make one feel uncomfortable—that is actually the culprit here.

Excessive fear is the main tool the ego uses to control and manipulate our consciousness. To justify inaction, the ego will spin tales of possible negative outcomes and "what ifs" if we start thinking of moving out of our comfort zone. Using fear-based scenarios, the ego will have us avoid being vulnerable in the context of relationships, ensuring we keep our walls up. Depending on whom it compares itself to, the ego will have us feeling inferior or superior, which is not only based in fear but separation as well.

With clarity and understanding, one can awaken to the fact that fear begins with a thought or an image in the mind. Because it's happening at the quantum level (the level of thought), it is at that level where it needs to be addressed and the root of fear needs to be pulled out. This process begins by understanding that fear is an illusion because the source of it is just that. The ego is a collection of changing and often incessant thought forms relative to the unchanging, eternal nature and formlessness of inner stillness. Fear, from a spiritual vantage point, is not real unless you give belief to it. And therein lies your free will. You are free to believe in whatever you want. It's only our identification with automatic thought, with ego, and innocently so, that has convinced us into believing we are limited, small, or less than.

Realizing that fear is not real is a large part of the awakening process—of coming into alignment with the sixth chakra—the third eye. All this is just a shift in perception and a shift in power. The shift is from believing fearful thoughts are real to seeing them clearly through elevated awareness as projected illusions. The effect of realizing this is reclaiming your power, which is your vital energy. Because you're no longer reacting to fear and wasting your precious energy and time, you start the process of coming back into balance. You shift into the centeredness of your inner being and its high vibrating energies.

The conscious approach that I have realized, which has been life-changing for me, is to observe automatic thought and the fear it supplies rather than react to it. Understanding that I have the personal power to call forth my reality has given me the clarity and knowing not to react to fear but instead starve it of my energy and power. With practice, one can move closer and closer toward mastery, where observing the thinking mind becomes second nature—where a fearful thought doesn't even have the momentum any longer to become a full-blown negative emotion or snowball into panic or dread.

Because fear is experienced within our minds, we can unconsciously choose to react to it or consciously cut it off from our supply of energy through awareness. Be mindful that being nonreactive to fear has nothing to do with suppressing negative emotion whatsoever. What is being done is quite the opposite of suppression. Instead, the fear that has been allowed to repeat itself is finally being given a send-off—a place to die, in a sense. By starving the ego of our energy, the authentic self (the soul) can come to life. As the ego is allowed to die, in an energetic sense, by letting things go—which is a large part of shadow work—your spiritual self is allowed to shine through. This process also brings to life all the spiritual gifts that come with it, such as powerful intuition, discernment, peace, and so forth. It's important to mention that your inner being is more than capable of dissolving any negativity or fear simply through its own presence when we are in conscious alignment with it. There is no darkness that can withstand the power of love when one is centered in their beingness through the present moment because it emanates from Source.

With a greater understanding of fear and how to approach it consciously, now's as good a time as ever to introduce an awareness-building exercise that will assist you in recognizing negative thinking at the onset, to cut it off from building momentum. The ability to discern a negative thought or emotion is key in allowing you to remain centered amidst fear and uncomfortable feelings. As awareness is cultivated, we in turn invite presence—the presence of our inner being—which emanates strength, stability, and fearlessness.

Just before we get into the exercise, let's look at ways that fear and negativity present themselves. For example, fear can appear as doubt, worry, anxiety, uncertainty, and a lack of trust. Essentially, it is based in some kind of potential loss. This fear of loss can surround a relationship, a financial issue, or a health matter, just to name a few. Negativity appears often as judgment anytime the ego is allowed to project and paint something or someone in a certain way. Emotions such as anger, guilt, and jealousy are lower-vibrating energies and are negative but serve as reminders or signals that you've come out of alignment. We've been conditioned to believe that we are our emotions, when in fact, they are messengers, not who we are but what we experience. What should also be mentioned regarding negative thinking is that when belief is given and resonated with, the only person being limited is ourselves. When we believe that life is unfair, that things never work out, or that we can't move forward, we're not only projecting negativity but also affirming our self-created limitations that are based out of the past. What fuels and perpetuates negative thinking and beliefs is the consistent referring to previous data for identity and giving it authority to dictate our present and future. With that being said, let's dive into the exercise.

Awareness-Building Exercise

You only need to set aside ten minutes or so for this exercise. You can begin doing this exercise once weekly, building up to two to three times a week, as you feel comfortable. Through practice, there is the possibility that awareness is so cultivated that you operate from this expanded state of awareness on a moment-by-moment basis.

You will need a piece of paper and a pen, or an electronic device. Find a quiet space and get comfortable. Once you're settled, start by taking three to four minutes bringing your awareness to the thinking mind. Simply observe the thoughts being presented.

After observing the thoughts for a few minutes, ask yourself the following questions:

- Were these thoughts positive, negative, or neutral?
- Did they feel fear-based or were they inspiring or uplifting?
- Were they coming from the past or being projected into the future?

Spend three or four minutes reflecting on the thoughts you experienced and write down your answers.

Once your answers are written down, briefly examine what you've written for the next few minutes, discerning what most of the thoughts were—positive or negative. Remember there are no right or wrong answers here.

The goal of this exercise is to invite greater awareness to the thinking mind, which will bring clarity. The more greater awareness and clarity is cultivated, the more empowered you'll become at discerning and diffusing negativity as it arises. By choosing to observe negativity, rather than react and identify with it, you will automatically raise your vibrational frequency in the process.

Challenging Negativity

Building upon the awareness exercise, let's lay a foundation as we move toward the next exercise, the third eye–activating exercise, which challenges negative thinking and/or feelings. We'll begin with some insights as to the importance of challenging negativity. We've been conditioned to react and project through ego identification. When the ego reacts and projects negative thoughts, it directs that negativity ultimately toward its host—you—even when the projection appears to be directed outwardly, toward something or someone else. Negativity is aways returned because the truth of the matter is that we're all one; all of life is a mirror. The same goes for positivity—when we extend high-vibrating, positive thoughts, we immediately receive them because although there seem to be many of us, there's really only one of us. It's all Source.

Another reason to challenge negative thinking/feelings is that it meets the ego's negativity with positivity, creating energetic balance in the moment. Challenging negativity invokes the conscious mind, awakening us from within. By affirming a positive thought, we shift our focus and set a course toward greater tranquility. The practice of challenging negative thinking creates an energetic momentum, one that is positive and energy shifting.

As you affirm a positive thought, it's important to be mindful of a few things. As you think or say out loud the positive thought, do so from the awareness of the present moment, hence the use of "I am" as you affirm. When you use the "I am" in challenging negative thinking, you are becoming that which you affirm *now* because everything, in fact, is taking place in the present. Remember also that the positive thought you're choosing is not based on past data but what you're deciding upon now. Lastly, you want to affirm the positive thought with belief, but even better yet, with knowing. Know that what you're affirming is a reality now, as you let go of how and when. This cultivates the power of your will.

We're now going to look at ten examples of negative thoughts/ feelings, and the affirming positive, vibration-shifting thoughts you can use to challenge them. As you begin to resonate with these life-affirming, positive thoughts, you may find that you attract more of the same. Remember that these positive thoughts are not based on current conditions but are sourced from the potential of the surrounding unified field—where all things are possible. Feel free to come up with more positive thinking as you see fit.

Positive Thoughts to Challenge Negativity

Negative Thought	Challenging Positive Thought
Things are never going to change.	Things are changing, and I am already seeing it take place.
I'm feeling stuck.	I am unstuck now and moving forward.
I'm always just scraping by.	I am abundant and recognize the abundance in my life.
I'm sad.	This is a temporary feeling; I am choosing happiness now.

Negative Thought	Challenging Positive Thought
I'm feeling anxious.	I am remembering the present moment, where peace resides.
I don't see life getting better.	Nothing is concrete; I am seeing improvement every day.
I have no motivation.	I am taking inner/outer action now; change begins with me.
I keep getting sick.	I am whole and healthy, stronger every day.
I'm mentally exhausted and tired.	I am renewed in mind, body, and spirit now.
I don't see hope in anything…	All of life is for me; I am seeing a wonderful life unfolding now.

Third Eye Activating Exercise

Building on the Awareness-Building Exercise, this exercise is aimed at activating and working with the third eye as you challenge negativity. A powerful energy-shifting spiritual faculty, the third eye is our imagination generator that also plays a key role in realizing greater potentials, which are reflections of higher vibrational or expanded states of consciousness. This practice is a large part of creating inner balance—meeting negativity with positivity by working with the conscious mind. Set ten to fifteen minutes aside for this exercise.

Find a quiet space and get comfortable.

Eyes can be open or closed. Take a few deep breaths and drop your shoulders as you relax into the moment. Before you begin, be mindful that thoughts—even negative ones—are just energy, and they don't have any power over you without your permission, which is only granted with your belief in them.

Begin by bringing your awareness to the thinking mind. As you do so, discern the thoughts that are negative or fear-based, as the focus is on challenging negative thinking. Do you notice a negative thought that's been persistent or reoccurring? Has there been a thought or a feeling that's been making you feel stuck? Spend five minutes bringing your awareness inward as you do this.

Once you've recognized a negative thought, observe it; just be witness to it. Then challenge it with a conscious thought that represents who you are now. For example, if the negative thought presents as a feeling of lack, dismiss it through observation, and then think or say out loud, "I am abundant, now and always." If you're being offered confusion regarding what steps to take next, respond with, "I am clarity, and I am being divinely guided."

Practice challenging negative thinking for the next five minutes. Be mindful that as you're affirming a positive, desirable thought, do so from an awareness that it's happening now—this is affirmed when you start a positive thought with "I am."

After spending a few minutes challenging negative thinking, take a few deep breaths and come back to the moment. The inner action of challenging negative thinking, of meeting negativity with positive, conscious thoughts, aligns you with the power of the third eye. The more you practice and do this inner work, the greater clarity you will have and the easier it will become for you. The third eye has the potential to fully open and silence negativity altogether, and working with it through this exercise can potentially set the stage for a spontaneous third eye activation: spiritual awakening.

This exercise can be practiced two to three times a week, to start. Increase the frequency as you feel comfortable. Through repetition, the spiritual skill of observing and then challenging negative thinking can become second nature and an empowering response leading to greater peace and well-being.

Roadblock: Repeating the Past, Projecting into the Future

The main reason we often feel stuck, sad, anxious, and like we're not getting ahead is the conditioned mind's one and only playbook of repeating past events, feelings, and experiences that are then projected into a supposed future. Hindering our potential, it primarily accomplishes this by suppressing and depressing our vibrational frequency—affecting how we feel—about ourselves, others, and life in general. Because of its nature, the ego accumulates negative energy over time, clinging to negative energies because that's what it is: attachment. Not wanting to let go, it traps negative emotions, causing tension within the mind and the body. Allowed to grow and accumulate, suppressed emotions can develop into depressed states that can leave us feeling "less than" unmotivated and cloud our perception, all of which impact one's outlook on life.

Operating through this lower-vibrating field—the past—is what allows it to be projected and perpetuated into the future. Belief in the past makes it seem real. And because the past has been given our belief and constant attention, it has been allowed to live through us, robbing us of our precious energy, as it prevents us from realizing a more fulfilled life. My goal in revealing this to you is to assist you in your own shadow work. Because self-awareness, understanding the way in which we've been operating, is key in undoing it, in healing and moving forward. It's also to spark an awakening within you, or if you're already in process of awakening, to further you along your evolutionary journey.

Solution: Seeing the Past and Future Differently

Awakening to the only moment there ever is—the present—offers you the clarity to perceive the past and the future differently. This is the beginning of personal liberation from the repetitive and incessant nature of the thinking mind. The past has always unfolded in the present. It's experienced in the mind as images and feelings such as sadness, regret, even the reflection of "better or happier times," all of which attempt to diminish the present moment. The future never arrives, being only experienced as thought projections, anticipation, excitement, but also as worry and anxiety.

Bringing awareness and presence to these mental constructs begins to create space and stillness between you and the ego. The key to reclaiming your power, the now, is the doorway back to the soul—your inner being. Anchoring your awareness in the present connects you with higher, elevating energies that the ego finds unpalatable. That's because the energies that are emitted from the present come from a higher dimension—the spiritual realm. These uplifting energies come as bliss, joy, happiness, and gratitude, which are all attributes of the soul.

The key is to become an observer of the past and the future—no longer a reactor to it. When you observe negativity, you are in alignment with your inner being, the silent self. Your inner being is nonattached because it knows it's one with everything and everyone. It knows nothing can be added to it because it's already whole and complete. The gift that comes with shifting your perception regarding the past and the future is that you'll still be able to experience these constructs, but you're no longer attached or controlled by them. You can see them for what they are. No longer a source of your suffering, these thought forms become reminders to reawaken to the present moment. Emotions that no longer serve you are dismissed and dissolved in the presence of your inner being—it's that powerful.

As you shift your inner perception, you realize your spiritual essence is experiencing human life. The past and the future are now used as sifting tools to what it is you prefer as well as differing perspectives. You're no longer fighting against the dark but rather taking away its power over your mind, which is the end of inner conflict, as peace is allowed to blossom the more you remember your ally that is the present moment.

Roadblock: Focusing on Circumstances

Focusing on externals and circumstances in turn makes things seem very concrete and "a matter of fact" rather than responsive to our vibrational frequency and intentions. Our human tendency is to be fixated on the surface, which keeps us from realizing what's truly important: reconnecting with our inner being and all its potential. The ego is always creating the idea that something's missing or lacking, making its purpose to always somehow diminish one's current reality by devaluing it.

The ego is also in and of itself resistance. Failing to see the abundance that is already present and unable to trust the process because of its nature, it can only paint what it focuses upon in darker tones. The thinking mind is the source for unhappiness and inner conflict, and it seeks to create problems in your mind by attempting to often convince you that your circumstances are unsatisfactory and cannot change—appearing permanent. It accomplishes this by focusing on "what is" and repeating what you see "out there" in your mind. This is what often leads to suffering and, for many, the feeling of being stuck.

Solution: Seeing Things with Clarity

Circumstances have no meaning save the meaning you give them. Everything is neutral until a label or a judgment is placed upon it. What you entertain within your mind is what is experienced as reality when it is given belief. What you focus upon expands, which then creates a feeling or an emotion, which impacts your vibrational frequency. If allowed to build momentum, one single resistant thought can develop into anger, resentment, fear, and inner conflict. This takes place when outer reality is allowed to be repeated in the inner. It's what happens when we fail to see that everything in life is temporal and temporary.

The empowering approach to any circumstance is to take a step back and observe it—remove all labels or judgments attached to it. This involves engaging the conscious mind, the awakened part of you. As you do this, you may almost immediately begin to feel some relief in the form of less tension in the physical body. Remembering that everything is experienced in your mind and that what you focus upon calls forth your reality, you instead consciously choose to reclaim your creative power and peace through nonreaction, responding instead. We all have preferences, and that's very much okay. Finding yourself in a situation or a place you don't want to be in or remain is the needed contrast to spark desire—the first step in setting a new course and intention.

Choosing to be grateful and looking for things to appreciate is what shifts you energetically, thereby setting the stage for something new. The higher energies of gratitude allow you to see the outer more clearly—as it is. Applying this conscious approach turns the table on narrow perspectives. It allows you to transcend the situation, inviting greater harmony to unfold. Now that you understand that all of life is a mirror, decide and then take the inner and outer action needed to change that which you find undesirable or what you've outgrown. Surrendering resistance, seeing things as neutral, and envisioning that which you desire, as you feel its manifested reality now, will inspire you to move forward. It will grant you the permission to take the action to marry the idea to physical reality.

Roadblock: Impatience and Waiting

What we resonate with energetically is what we become—in the moment. The thoughts and energies that are currently being entertained in our vibrational field shift us into a reality—although subtle—that reflects what we're being. This happens countless times a day, usually without one's conscious awareness. The reason I bring this up is because the energies of "I can't wait until it finally happens" and "I'm waiting for it to manifest" or "I've been waiting so long for it to come" and "Why is it taking so long?" all shift you into a state of impatience and waiting. This train of thought, if allowed to be repeated day in and day out, will keep you in a continuous cycle of waiting. This attachment/negative energy diminishes one's journey toward the destination or desire.

Life is now. Source is now. Your inner being that is already in alignment with every desire you could ever imagine is right here, right now. We miss the point when we get caught up in achieving and attaining, overlooking what's most important, which is knowing who one is spiritually. What I'm getting at is that every wish and desire is already within your energetic field, as it's a reflection of your inner being. Waiting for some future moment for fulfillment, happiness, or satisfaction will just keep you waiting. The interesting thing is that when you shift out of the energies of impatience and waiting, you allow what's already a 5D reality to manifest that much more smoothly and efficiently as you instead come from a space of nonresistance.

Solution: Releasing Resistance

The key to not only allowing your desires to manifest without delay but also enjoying the process along the way is the concept of letting go. Allow me to explain. When we finally let go of the inner conflict and resistance due to fear and doubt, we allow peace back into our minds. When we let go of the belief that life is a struggle, we experience flow. And when we finally surrender all our life's affairs—which includes our desires—to Source, we shift into an expanded version of ourselves, one that is in alignment with the forward movement of life. We don't have to struggle, but we are free to do so, if we choose. We don't have to keep waiting for the feelings of happiness, fulfillment, and joy through outer attachments—we can choose those feelings right now. By choosing them, by embodying those energies.

The soul (your inner being) is spontaneous by nature and is the source of miracles in your life. Getting into alignment with it shifts you into a space of potential where anything can happen at any time. This can include, but is not limited to, a spontaneous awakening; a spontaneous healing; or a moment where you receive a flash of genius or insight, an answer to a question you've been wanting, or a sudden shift where you are experiencing one form or various forms of abundance. There are no limits to what your inner being can accomplish—you just have to get out of the way by freeing yourself of the energies that are cutting you off from directly experiencing it. Know that what you truly seek and desire is to be free of fear and all its branching emotions. To accomplish this, you must let go of who you thought you were and allow the authentic you—your soul—to express itself as the fearlessness and knowingness it is. When you let it all go, you allow everything to come in—this is the art of nonattachment.

Roadblock: Fear of the Unknown

What keeps many of us stuck from elevating in consciousness is not knowing what's beyond fear and our human conditioning. The question of what would happen if one were to let go, stop worrying, and refrain from anticipating and self-sabotaging through self-made negative prophesies is a powerful one. It's one that needs reflecting on.

One of the issues that many of us face is that we've become too complacent and comfortable with our fears and pain. The reason behind the complacency and comfortableness is that it's all too familiar—it's known in a sense but not really understood. When fear is allowed to keep us in check, we will self-sabotage relationships, ideas, and dreams, often before they're even given a chance to get off the ground. The projected fear that "the past will just be repeated" is an example of a seed—a thought energy—that's powerful enough to stop one from taking action and moving forward toward a desire.

The ego by nature is controlling, always wanting to control the situation and even others. The reason it operates this way is because of the fear of loss—of potentially losing something, such as pride, or someone. Yet it's this very same energy that is contradictory to life and that repels things and people. You can look at all the layers of the ego, but every layer will always turn out to be the same: fear in one form or another. It's this low-vibrating energy that must be looked at consciously and transcended through awareness to move forward.

Solution: Cultivating Faith and Trust

Automatically believing what is experienced within the mind brings involuntary faith and trust in fear, which is our biggest roadblock. You're not lacking faith or trust; it's just been misdirected. The solution is to take back your faith and trust in it and place it deeper inward—toward your inner being, toward Source and life itself. An excellent way to cultivate faith and trust is to briefly look back and reflect on a time in your life where there seemed no way, and yet a way was made out of a sticky situation. Life or Source just needs the opportunity to show you what's possible, but it's going to take the relinquishing of your faith and trust in fear.

This inner conscious action involves not automatically believing what the thinking mind presents to you. It also entails working with the conscious mind and affirming positive thoughts and words such as: "I am no longer placing automatic belief in fear," "I am letting go and trusting the process," "I have faith in myself and in Source," and "I trust I am always being divinely guided." This inner shift in recognizing the fear-dismantling power in these divine potentials elevates your vibrational frequency and invites relief. As you become open to more desirable experiences by negating worry, you untie the universe's hands in the process. As you cultivate and practice bringing to life these powerful forces in a positive way, you will find that faith and trust will serve you well—you just need to cultivate trusting the process.

What should also be mentioned is that the conscious local mind is designed only to direct your intentions and be aware of the here and now. The higher mind or the highest self knows what's ahead, knows the path moving forward toward your desires and communicates to you via intuition, energetic nudges, and inspiration to guide you to act. Your job is not to know every step but rather to become clear and begin vibrating at the frequency of your desires through conscious inner and outer action. It's up to us to pay attention to the subtle and not-so-subtle cues and synchronicities. Know that a way has been made; you just have to align with it in mind, body, and soul. This alignment begins with awareness, which will translate to clarity, which will allow you to remember and cultivate the spiritual forces of faith and trust.

Roadblock: The Idea of Victimhood

I think most, if not all, of us can attest to being a victim of repeating patterns of thought at one time or another. The contracting self-talk of "why does this keep happening to me?" closes us off from realizing we are the cause of our effects. When we operate this way, we are not only telling the universe "I am powerless" but we're also inviting more future life experiences of the same because it's all based on vibrational frequency—what we're resonating with. Making the simple shift to "what is the purpose of this?" or "what is the lesson in this?" opens the door to potential answers and insight, which can invite direction that can help one move forward.

Solution: Shift from "Why" to "What"

The shift to "what is this situation or circumstance trying to tell me?" Invites the conscious mind into the mix, opening the door to answers. When we have repeating, undesired scenarios—be it in relationships or finances, for example—we need to look at our core beliefs surrounding these facets of our lives. From an energetic and manifesting perspective, it's not so important what you've been through, moving forward, but what you're being now. When things are continuously repeated in our lives it's because there's an underling issue—a thought or belief is at play in the background. Cultivating mindfulness through quiet meditation, bringing our attention to the higher mind (stillness) for its perspective and looking for the meaning within the message will offer clarity sooner or later. One thing is certain—it will always arrive when you're ready to receive, in divine timing.

Life is one of our greatest teachers, and it provides us with many experiences and lessons in the process. Becoming aware that everything and everyone is a messenger in some way invites insight and understanding. Negative or undesirable experiences are asking us to look within—find the underlying energy that's causing the vibrational frequency that's aligning with repeating lessons. It's important to remember that nothing is ever being done to us—but for us—to awaken us. This shift in perception has us moving from feeling a victim to our negative thoughts to a more conscious version of ourselves, one that can discern the message or lesson being offered that simultaneously allows for growth and further maturity.

Projection Is Energetic Self-Attack

Projection, which is the ego's mode of operation, works in limiting, bombarding, and blocking the chakras with negative emotion. This perspective is important and crucial to examine because it sheds light on our human conditioning and negative patterns, making it possible to see ourselves more clearly, giving us the insight to make inner corrections and shift forward in a more empowered and positive way. This is a large part of shadow work—to be able to face with discernment the energetic roadblocks that have created layers of emotional density that have generated a sense of separation between our awareness and our spiritual nature and the healing experienced within it. In this very important section, we'll put negative emotion under a magnifying glass, revealing its impact on the chakra system when it goes unresolved, creating energetic imbalances.

The negative emotion being projected outward is what determines the chakra that will be impacted. Just as there are positive expressions that emanate from each chakra, causing us to expand and grow, negative emotions contract and limit the subtle body's energy wheels. We're now going to look at each chakra and some of the more pervasive corresponding negative emotions/feelings and the underlying limiting beliefs that create imbalance within them.

Chakra	Negative Emotions/Feelings	Limiting Beliefs
Root	Feeling insecure, chronic fear, sense of lack, instability, not trusting the process, feeling blocked, a sense of imbalance	"I feel stuck," "I don't trust anyone," and "I'm on shaky ground."
Sacral	Fear of intimacy, feeling uninspired, lack of creativity, feeling unfulfilled, lacking boundaries, feeling uncertain, guilt	"I feel unattractive," "I'm just not creative," and "I feel empty."
Solar Plexus	Feelings of frustration, helplessness, victimhood, lack of confidence, hanging on to past criticism, feeling powerless, not wanting to take responsibility	"Everything always happens to me," "I can't change," and "Nothing ever works out."
Heart	Lack of self-love, feeling undeserving, grief, feeling lonely, sadness, difficulty forgiving oneself/others, feelings of hatred	"I hate my life," "I'm unworthy," and "I just can't/don't know how to forgive."

Chakra	Negative Emotions/Feelings	Limiting Beliefs
Throat	Low self-esteem, fear of expression, negative or limiting self-talk, fear of rejection, inability to self-express, fear of public speaking, feelings of being unheard	"I'm always being judged," "Nobody ever listens to me," "Sharing how I feel will jeopardize this relationship."
Third Eye	Anxiety, self-doubt, feeling disconnected from your intuition, indecisive, close-minded, negative outlook, feeling a lack of clarity	"Nothing makes sense," "I'm a failure," and "The world is a scary place."
Crown	Belief in separation, attachment, material focused, lack of purpose, feeling disconnected from one's spiritual self, feelings of boredom, being unable to let go	"I don't know what to do with my life," "I get bored easily," and "I don't know who I am."

Bringing the dark to light through self-reflection brings us clarity and direction, a road map to resolving the underlying energetic block that is impacting not only the particular chakra but also our well-being. Healing starts with self-awareness and understanding how we got to where we are and why we feel the way we do. With this approach, we can set a new course and know how to face future challenges with greater discernment, thereby knowing how to shift ourselves more quickly and effectively back into balance.

By recognizing the negative energies or feelings we experience, we can piece together the negative beliefs that stem from those emotions. Understanding that we're working with energy, positive and negative, we can work with negative feelings and emotions, transmuting them rather than perpetuating them. As you become more aware of the branching limiting beliefs that stem from negative emotion, you can consciously choose to challenge them, replacing them with higher, more empowering life-affirming thoughts. The cultivation of mindfulness and becoming aware of the shadow self or ego, shifts you from being an unconscious participant to a conscious responder. The first perpetuates negativity and feelings of hopelessness, while the latter renews one, inspiring you to move forward and take the necessary inner and outer action.

THREE Root Chakra: *Ground Yourself*

Chakra work begins by laying a foundation, and a strong one at that. We begin by anchoring our awareness and grounding ourselves into the present moment because the now is crucial in facing and transmuting fear. Fear creates instability, the feeling of being stuck, and other insecurities such as self-doubt and self-esteem issues. The more you remember the present moment and operate with the awareness of it, the more presence—your inner being—you align with. Surprisingly, ascending in consciousness is facilitated by deepening your connection to the lowest chakra, the one closest to Mother Earth. This grounding provides the necessary stability and strength for spiritual liftoff.

Being grounded in the root chakra centers you energetically and allows you to be rooted in beingness, making the human experience more meaningful through authentic and compassionate engagement. The element of earth, which represents the first chakra, serves as your bedrock from which you can lay the groundwork for personal fulfillment and growth. Growing in awareness brings you more in alignment with your highest self and purpose while inviting high-vibrating energies to raise you in consciousness, up through the chakras.

As the root chakra becomes activated and is allowed to harness more universal energy, the more stability you will experience, as well as the feeling of being grounded and empowered to navigate life and its challenges. The awareness of being grounded in the now makes you feel rock solid, as it is unchanging, steadfast, and unmovable. Being deeply anchored in your root chakra as you embody its characteristics affords you the clarity and discernment moving forward to recognize fear as it arises and approach it consciously through a spirit of fearlessness.

We're going to look at ways to deepen your connection with the root chakra and the signs that will tell you that you're activating and opening it. A large part of any inner work is awareness because it's our very own awareness that gives life to a concept or an idea. We're always operating through and with universal energy—the very energy that is the source of life.

Five Ways to Connect Deeper with the Root Chakra

- Take two or three minutes daily to imagine and feel your connectedness with Mother Earth.
- As you wake up, affirm: "I am grounded in my root chakra, and I am safe, stable, and secure, now and always."
- Unplug from the busyness of life by spending time in nature—walking or meditating. The key is to be present.
- Make a practice of challenging negative thinking, as it will enable a positive outlook on life.

- Remember who you are in spirit, in Source. This is an excellent way to align with the power and strength of the soul, which is the source of the chakras.

Signs You're Activating and Opening the Root Chakra

- You feel calmer and more centered, even amidst uncomfortable feelings.
- Greater clarity is being experienced, as you're able to discern more between fear and inspiration.
- You have an overall greater sense of well-being and increased mental strength and vitality.
- Your awareness is more anchored in the present moment, and you're becoming more of an observer of the past and future. This inner awareness is stabilizing, as you're less swayed by the back-and-forth motion of the thinking mind.
- A greater sense of inner peace is felt as your deeper connection with spirit reflects that.

Maintaining Balance

We have many tools and strategies at our disposal that can assist us in maintaining inner balance. Inner balance is a continuous process that requires our conscious involvement; we must be an active participant in our vital energy maintenance. It's all about pluses and minuses and meeting our unconscious aspect with our awakened conscious mind so that our inner flow of energy can move unrestricted as well-being is cultivated. Resistance and fear bottleneck the flow of universal energy, and the perpetuation of negativity is the only thing standing between you and realizing your highest self and all its potential.

Thankfully, with awareness and some consistent inner and outer action, we can approach the shadow self and its trappings in an empowered way—one where change takes place as soon as a different thought is chosen. Shifting our focus is one of the main ways to maintain inner balance. It's our decision to focus upon and feed fear and the "what ifs" that has allowed imbalance to take place within our vibrational frequency. Responding to fear with an unafraid spirit, one that sees fear for what it is, is what centers us in our divinity. There are other insights that one can remember daily and strategies that can be employed that can not only help maintain inner balance but also shift you into more high-vibrating and positive states. Let's look at four balance-creating approaches that will serve you and shift you into higher energetic states.

Challenge Negative Thinking

Our human conditioning is what automatically offers us negative thoughts, contracting emotions, and even a less desirable outlook. The ego is designed to operate this way because without all its contrast, we couldn't awaken to our light and appreciate who and what we really are. To bring balance to the ego's negativity, we must introduce positive thoughts, higher-vibrating feelings, or states of being and consciously choose our outlook by first remembering we are powerful manifesters who call forth our reality through our vibrational frequency. Remembering that it's our inner world that reflects the outer, we remind ourselves how vital it is to meet fear with fearlessness, the unconscious aspect of ourselves with the conscious, awakened mind. When presented with a limiting or fearful thought *we have time to choose differently* because of our experience of space-time. Choosing a more desirable and positive thought with belief or better yet, with knowing, shifts you into a more positive state.

Experiencing higher-vibrating feelings/states of being is also just an intention away by choosing what we feel consciously—by becoming what we express, such as "I am happy" or "I am peace and joy." The momentum of positive thinking and consciously choosing how we feel sets the stage for a more positive outlook because we are deciding where we are headed, rather than being directed by negative emotion or external forces. Deciding that "life keeps getting better and better" or "things are unfolding in my favor" shifts one's outlook on life more positively, to say the least.

Remember the Here and Now

The belief and identifying with the past and the future are what create energetic imbalances within us. Becoming aware of and aligning consciously with the eternal moment of now shifts us into higher-vibrating energies, which bring balance automatically. Consciously resonating with the present aligns us closer with our inner being, which expresses clarity, insights, wisdom, and understanding—all gifts meant to guide us and assist us in navigating our lives. Becoming more present-moment aware also allows us to remember what's really important—makes our priorities clear—which assists us in balancing our lives overall.

Be Preemptive in Your Positive Thinking

Choosing conscious, positive thoughts at the beginning of the day and expressing them as you go about your day, sets the stage from the time you wake up and creates positive momentum. By operating in this fashion, you can create so much positive energy that when faced with a dilemma or a stressful situation, the already-created and supportive energies can not only assist you in navigating through the challenge but also have you move past it more efficiently. Choosing positive thoughts, such as "all is well," "everything always works out for me," or "I am more than capable," shifts you into a more empowered version of yourself—one that is more balanced, centered, and clear.

Operate from a Space of Gratitude

Gratitude is a powerful energy to embody. Being grateful raises your vibrational frequency and opens the door to more things for you to become grateful for. Expanding and inviting, gratitude is an attitude that moves effortlessly with the forwardness of life, allows for different forms of abundance, and just feels good. Being in the space of gratitude shifts one from the lower energies of resentment and frustration to happiness and joy. Those who choose gratitude daily and consistently are consciously manifesting their destiny. They've remembered who they are and their potential to call forth their desired life consciously.

Shadow Work Prompts: Addressing Specific Root Chakra Blocks

A large part of shadow work is being able to recognize the core issues that are causing the negative thoughts and feelings being experienced. By becoming aware of the negativity, we're able to take directed inner and outer action to bring about a resolution and healing. The process of healing and achieving and maintaining inner balance is an ongoing process—one of mindful awareness and discernment. The following energetic blocks are meant to shine a spotlight on some of the main challenges we experience as humans. Because the issues are of a mental and energetic nature, they require a conscious and energetic approach. Let's begin:

Feeling Insecure

Comparison is a thief, and when we compare ourselves with others, it's because we've forgotten who we are in Source. As spiritual beings navigating human existence, we each possess unique strengths and weaknesses. It's our differences that give us the experience of contrast and relativity—this experience we call life abounds in it. Unconsciously permitting our attention to focus on others and what they have that we don't throws us off center, making us feel less than. Focusing on the external world amplifies it within our minds, making things seem even greater than they really are.

Inner Work: Recognize that whenever your attention is focused externally and you start comparing yourself to others, it's your forgetfulness of your uniqueness driving that unconscious comparison. The key is to become aware when you feel comparison taking place and then making the conscious choice to dismiss it by remembering everyone is experiencing their own personal and unique timeline. Embracing and celebrating your unique qualities, finding value in your personal perspectives and strengths, shifts you away from the need for comparison. The following affirmations provide balancing energies to the feeling of being insecure by reminding you of who you are in spirit. Be mindful that these affirmations are not based on the past but what you're free to choose now.

Affirmations: "I am secure and confident within myself," "I am centered in my beingness," and "I am strong and capable."

Chronic Fear and Anxiety

We've all, at one time or another, experienced fear and the worry or anxiety that comes with it. When we dwell on and feed imagined negativity, anxiety can take root and negatively influence other areas of our lives. But know that even then, longtime fears can be healed in an instant with a moment of clarity, as there is no time in the spiritual realm that surrounds us. Being fearful and anxious bottlenecks universal energies and throws us off center, leaving us susceptible to lower-vibrating energies that create root chakra imbalances.

Inner Work: Because fear and anxiety are based in the future, caused by experience, the solution is to remember and come back to the safety, certainty, and stability of the present moment. Your highest self, which is fearless, understands what fear is but will never identify with nor yield to it. Let it be your guiding light out of the darkness by deeply reflecting on the last sentence as you remember that you're an extension of the highest self.

Understanding that the past and the future offer unique perspectives and are not who we are reveals that we don't have to take them so seriously. Becoming aware of and focusing on the high-vibrational energy of the now aligns you with the inner peace and balance of your higher-dimensional self, which is always present. The practice of being mindful throughout the day, especially when limiting or fearful thoughts attempt to predict and limit your future, assists you in remaining clear and balanced as you navigate your day.

Being one with the present moment is tantamount to a form of energy medicine, where awareness itself automatically applies soothing and healing energies. A result of being present and grounded in the now automatically connects you with the root chakra, further rooting you into spirit and the peace that it reflects as a quiet mind. The affirming intentions offered next are designed to remind and realign you with your inner being, who is present-moment focused and fearless.

Affirmations: "I am fearless now and always," "I am comfortable amidst uncomfortable feelings," and "I am one with the present moment."

Sense of Lack

The feeling of lack closes us off to the limitless abundance found within and around us, and in doing so, blocks the root chakra. When we're disconnected from our base or core beingness, the experience is one of confusion, as we are clouded to who and what we really are. Feeling that something is missing from within, that idea can then project itself onto our finances and even relationships. It is a self-sabotaging energy, and so like will attract like in this case. Overall, the root cause of a sense of lack is forgetting our oneness with Source, and with life itself.

Inner Work: Remembering one's interconnectedness, to Source, Mother Earth, and all of life, reminds us that we are one with it all. It's this remembrance that ushers in the truth of our inner being, dispelling the idea that we are lacking. Being mindful that everything is first experienced within, as a thought or emotion—positive or negative—clarifies that the solution is to apply spiritual awareness. Nothing lacks when you are connected and aware of your spiritual nature because your inner being is abundant in health, happiness, joy, peace, wisdom, clarity, and so on.

Even if on the surface there appears to be, for example, material lack, through inner alignment and changing your thoughts about the situation or circumstance, you shift from feeling like a victim to feeling like a conscious responder, which allows positive change to take place. The following affirmations are meant to remind you of your inner and outer abundance, as they meet feelings of lack with the potential and possibility of calling forth what is already here and now in the unseen.

Affirmations: "I am abundant now and always," "I lack nothing," and "Prosperity continuously flows to me."

Experiencing Instability

The world around us is experienced within our minds, and it's vital that we live from a space that's balanced and stable so we can boldly traverse adversity. Being unprepared by not having a firm understanding of how energy and grounding works within us can leave us feeling like we're on shaky ground when faced with a sudden change in our life. This in turn can leave us experiencing confusion and resentment.

Another challenge we face in these modern times is information overload because of how easy it is to access news from a variety of sources. Overly consuming negative data, be it from television or the internet, with an unguarded mind can have a detrimental impact on our mental state, fostering feelings of anger and even hopelessness. Leaving our emotions and well-being at the mercy of outer forces can also lead to unhappiness and a diminished sense of control over our lives.

Inner Work: One of the ways you can start creating less external dependence for the way you feel is to briefly examine how you've dealt with challenges and excess information in the past. Recognizing moments when you've felt instability is the first step in the process of building self-awareness. Those instances can provide insights and lessons if one is open to receive.

One of the lessons could be the reminder not to place all of one's happiness in the hands of others or even material possessions. Because being heavily invested in those things for our inner state of being leaves us defenseless when life throws us curveballs. Choosing to foster your well-being from the inside-out now by developing a positive, balanced mindset through positive intentions and different perspectives is an investment in your mental and spiritual health.

A conscious approach to information received as news or an online post involves reframing automatic belief and avoiding immediate absorption of the energies behind the information, as they are often fear-based. An online post from someone's social media account is just one perspective from a myriad of potential points of view. And news is always changing. The other important thing to mention is to give yourself breaks from the constant information being fed to you. You can give yourself certain times throughout the day where you turn away from electronics and just spend time being still, practicing mindfulness, or connecting with loved ones. Life is often hectic, and all its constant change requires us to go within and commune with the silent, unchanging nature of our inner being. True balance and stability come from doing the work in mind, body, and spirit. The following intentions will invite and direct stabilizing energies into your vibrational frequency.

Affirmations: "I am stable and secure," "I am anchored into the high-vibrating energies of the now," and "I am centered in my root chakra."

Not Trusting the Process

This stems from a misplacement of energy, which in this case is invested in fear and doubt rather than the highest self and the divine synchronistic unfolding of one's life. Our local conscious mind is not designed to know every step but rather is a means to experience the here and now. Know that when you're not trusting the process it's because you're still focused on unwanted things, which creates nonacceptance and the very obstacles you're desiring to move away from. Being in a non-trusting state cuts us off from the supporting energies and balance afforded from the root chakra—moving up. It shifts us from experiencing the natural joy, steadiness, and nonresistance and instead contracts our energy to resonate with dream-robbing energies. Thankfully, these energetic blocks can be resolved with some clarity, insight, and inner action.

Inner Work: Faith and trust are powerful forces that require some awareness and cultivation so that they can shift one toward higher states of consciousness and ultimately, one's highest potential. The decision to surrender to how and when the desire will manifest is freedom from the linear time attachments that are keeping the wish from coming into one's reality. Surrendering is a sign of spiritual maturity, one that recognizes the already built-in control that emanates from the highest self. True inner change takes place when we can look at life with total acceptance while knowing that everything is temporary and apt to change. Deciding to move forward with life regardless of what shows up is not only freeing but also expands your consciousness in the process, as you allow contracting and doubting energies to move through you. Making the conscious decision to trust the process and allow spiritual forces that are for you to bring you that which you desire clears your field of frustration, resentment, and anger. Asserting the following phrases assists you in energetically aligning with the forward current of life.

Affirmations: "I am surrendering to the life forces that are for me," "I am trusting the process moment by moment," and "I am choosing faith and trust over fear."

Feeling Stuck

Being out of alignment with the grounded energy provided through an activated and open root chakra has a negative impact on the other chakras. Being fearful and entertaining feelings of uncertainty consistently is what contracts and impedes the chakras—especially the root chakra—from functioning optimally. The perpetuation of negative states creates an environment that stifles one's potential and ability to make progress. Repetitive undesirable thoughts and feelings often manifest as recurring external experiences, potentially leaving individuals in a cycle of inner and outer stagnation. Being an energetic problem, it calls for an energetic solution, starting with awareness and some clarity.

Inner Work: The paradox is that you can only truly begin to move upward in consciousness and forward in life when your awareness is rooted in the present moment. Becoming unstuck begins by addressing the repeating fears and feelings one has been experiencing. For some, it's the fear of lack, fear of things being repeated, fear of the unknown, or the fear of failure. The perception of a lack of progress or the presence of unfulfilled desires can often lead to negative emotional states, which can further reinforce the feeling of being stuck in a rut. The result of this narrow outlook is trapped energy that keeps one in a loop. Recognizing that fear has no bite without your belief lays the road map on how to dissolve its grip on your consciousness while restoring a sense of progress.

The solution to resolving repetitive fears and feelings is to allow these trapped energies to move through you. This is accomplished by becoming impersonal toward them by looking at them without anything but awareness. You can choose to become unbothered by them and stand your ground because running away from them through avoidance is what perpetuates them. Decide to no longer be triggered by them and they will begin to lose their attachment to you. When one looks at anything in the mind or within the body fearlessly, the deeper part of us, *the Presence within*, is invited to come forward. Being the highest self, it's transformative by nature in that it alchemizes negativity because of its high vibrational frequency. Remembering that fear and negative feelings need to be approached with a calm quiet rather than worry will assist you in letting negative energies pass without much difficulty.

Returning to the centeredness of the root chakra and its grounding energies aligns you with the knowingness of spirit and intuitive guidance that's always being offered. By being rooted in your inner being—starting at the base—you allow potentials to come to life and inspiration to express, and you begin to dream a desired life. This inner shift toward stability sets the stage for positive change in the outer. Cultivating a forward-moving mindset requires direction, which is provided by the following declarations that ideally are backed by knowing and certainty.

Affirmations: "I am already moving forward in life," "I am unstuck now," and "I am flowing with forward-moving life energies."

Root Chakra Healing Meditation

The purpose of this guided meditation is to ground, center, activate, and open your root chakra. Keep in mind that whatever is experienced within the mind through intention is taking place in the higher dimensions—on an energetic level—now. With practice and by applying mindfulness techniques, such as remembering the now moment throughout the day, you can embody a more empowered, centered, and fearless version of yourself. You can begin with this meditation once to twice a week and then use it when needed to ground yourself. It should only take about ten minutes. To begin, find a quiet space and get comfortable, sitting or lying down. Close your eyes and take a few deep breaths as you relax into the moment. Drop your shoulders as you bring your awareness inward. Just before you start the meditation, remind yourself that the present moment is all there ever is.

Next, imagine yourself standing outside in a peaceful place amongst trees, barefoot on grass. The sun is shining, and the temperature is just right. Now imagine yourself feeling anchored to the ground as you feel strong and centered. As you're imagining this, see your root chakra appearing at the base of your spine. See it in your mind's eye as a red circular energy spinning clockwise at the perfect pace. Keep this image in your mind for the next three to four minutes as you breathe deeply and slowly.

For the next part of the meditation, spend the next minute or two envisioning the root chakra activating (see it beginning to glow a brighter red) and expanding, surrounding the center of your being. Once you've imagined this, let the image go, keeping your eyes closed. Express the affirmations by speaking the following three times, gently but with great certainty, feeling, and knowing: "I am grounded and centered in my root chakra. I am one with my inner being. I am anchored in the present moment now and always. My root chakra is activated and operating optimally now."

The meditation is now complete. Take a few deep breaths, open your eyes, and bring your awareness to your surroundings. Give thanks for root chakra healing and activation, as you remember that you're unconditionally supported.

General Root Chakra Healing

If you're still unclear as to what specific negative emotion/block is impacting the root chakra, you can approach healing and opening it in a more general sense. As you align more with this chakra and its consciousness, you will connect to it deeper, bringing to light what it requires from you, what issue needs addressing. Healing is not always in a direct, linear fashion and can at times redirect us, which can ultimately end up benefiting us even more later.

The experience of fear and the amount of life force we feed it—ranging from being slightly anxious to full-on panic—is reflected by just how grounded we are in our root chakra. The more you practice being mindful of the now and its higher-vibrating energies, and being centered in your beingness, the less impact fear will have on you. There are also other inner and outer actions you can take to starve fear, which will allow further healing to take place. We'll now look at five more ways to allow root chakra healing.

Five Ways to Allow Root Chakra Healing

- Cultivate self-responsibility and trust: An activated and open root chakra represents the ability to take care of ourselves—the ability to meet our own basic needs. Feeling secure within ourselves begins by trusting who we are and the decisions we make. This all starts by understanding and knowing our spiritual selves. The soul—who you are beyond thought—is not only trustworthy but also stable, secure, unafraid, and balanced. Making it a practice to know and remember one's spiritual nature through self-reflection and meditation empowers one to make responsible and clear choices—cultivating trust in oneself and the process. It's trust that starves fear, which permits universal energy to flow freely through the root chakra, reenergizing it as well as our subtle body in the process.
- Understanding what inner peace is and what it feels like gives us a baseline to understanding when we're out of balance, empowering us to take mindful action to come back to center. The peace of spirit reflects a quiet mind, and it's the direct experience of being one with our inner being: the soul. It's also faith and trust that's been cultivated that allows you to know a way has been made even if you don't quite yet see one. Every moment is an opportunity—the doorway back to the soul and one's conscious

awareness of it. It's where insights and intuition are more easily discerned, enabling our spiritual senses to guide us and remind us of our natural state of being, which is one of peace, calm, and serenity—all reflections of someone who is centered within themself.

- Practice being grounded. People who are grounded have made the choice to choose clarity and stability over confusion and imbalance. It is a continuous process, but one that pays dividends. Those who practice being present, focused, and self-aware are flexible in their thinking, have a more positive outlook on life, and can approach emotions in a more centered and conscious way. All of this is made possible when we are aware of our unconscious and conscious aspects.
- Living consciously from the inside-out allows greater balance and peace to unfold as we shift from being a reactor to the outside world to being a witness to it. The highest self doesn't judge or put a label on anything. In truth, nothing has any meaning of any kind until we place one. We decide if we live in a friendly and safe world or one of chaos and drama. The first is a conscious decision based on potential, and the latter is based on living from the past—what others have told us through direct and indirect ways. You get to decide and choose consciously what kind of world you want to live in. This is not only empowering but also grounding—one that sets the stage for future experience—within and without.
- Immerse yourself with nature inside the comfort of your own home. There are many benefits to having plants inside

your home, such as improved air quality and elevated mood levels. But there is also a deeper potential benefit that plants can offer with some awareness. Plants are masters of stillness by their very nature. Taking just a few minutes a day to focus our awareness on a plant can allow the stillness within and surrounding the plant to be reflected within us. This, in a way, is a form of meditation—it's focus on stillness. This simple practice is a great way to clear the mind and become centered, and it can assist one in becoming more in tune with mind, body, and spirit—the wholeness of who we are.

Being Grounded for Your Highest Timeline

When activated and open, your root chakra serves as a powerful portal, aligning you with higher timelines, miracles, and possibilities. The root chakra is the foundation of the chakra system and the rock from which to build a successful life. Being grounded and centered in your beingness sets the stage for an empowered version of yourself that has the clarity, insight, and strength to confidently manifest and navigate life. Being in alignment with this energy center is the connecting force to your highest self and all that it reflects, which allows you to embody fearlessness. It's this unafraid state of mind, one that has transcended fear, that invites the highest self to express itself as miracles, such as spontaneous healings or synchronicities and all the possibilities that are available within the unified field.

Your highest potential reflects your conscious awareness and embodiment of the highest self, Source within. An integration of mind, body, and spirit, every aspect of you is honored and utilized as a whole to bring beingness to doingness—the supernatural to the natural. An unblocked root chakra allows high-vibrating and free-flowing universal energy to move up toward the crown chakra, maintaining the upward and downward movement of energy to maintain inner balance and harmony. Being in this free-flowing state gives the clarity to make decisions and forge ahead. With this centeredness and focus, things like intuition, direction, and inspiration become more easily discernible from the highest self and your spirit guides.

Miracles are the status quo when one is aligned with their spiritual nature and aware of the surrounding unified field, not the exception. What should also be mentioned is that from the highest self's point of view, there are no differences or levels of difficulty in miracles; all being extensions of unconditional love, they have no limits in what they can achieve. From a spiritual vantage point, it's just as easy to manifest a dime or a dream home—levels of difficulty are only a conditioned point of view. Remembering that every moment is a miracle through awareness of the self allows life to unfold before your eyes in the most profound way; seeing beyond the surrounding material world, you recognize the unifying field that encompasses it all.

Operating beyond the confusion, doubt, and limitedness of fear, the potential and infinite possibilities that stem from your inner being come front and center. Understanding that all things are in fact possible, you begin to form a vision for your life. You dream bigger and imagine that which you once thought impossible, knowing that if it can be imagined, it already exists in the unseen spiritual realm. Understanding that the dreams for your life are inspired by the soul itself, you embody that which you desire to experience by thinking, speaking, and taking inspired action to merge the higher imagined state to your physical reality. It's this process that takes the awareness of one's highest self and allows it to be expressed as one's highest timeline or potential—in terms of state of mind, health, happiness, fulfillment, harmonious relationships, abundance, and so much more.

Inner Stability Exercise

The inner work of activating and energizing the root chakra is only an intention away. The mind is where we experience and bring to life that which we focus upon. What we envision through our mind's eye is what we call forth from the higher realms and into this one. It's important to be aware that when you are consciously intending something, know that it's done now—not in some future moment. Spirit is not limited by space-time because all of life—everything—is happening now.

This exercise needs only five minutes or so and can be practiced once weekly until you find yourself centered in your root chakra and deeply aware of the present. It can be referred to anytime you feel you're out of balance and have shifted your awareness away from the now moment. Find a quiet space and get comfortable, sitting or lying down. Close your eyes and take three to four deep breaths as you ease into the moment. As you come into a more relaxed state, drop your shoulders and remember you're in the here and now.

Now imagine yourself standing on a large, flat, red-earthy rock (which represents the root chakra) with the words *present moment* impressed on the front of it.

As you imagine this, feel yourself being centered and anchored on top of the rock. See ascending energies rising from the ground, surrounding and supporting you. As you're imagining these high-vibrating energies of golden light, see the following words swirling up and around you: *strength, stability, supported, fearless, centered,* and *abundant.*

Hold this image for the next three or four minutes and feel the gratitude now for the feeling of being strong, stable, unconditionally supported, fearless, centered, and abundant.

After holding this image in your mind for a few minutes, take a few deep breaths, then let the image go. Open your eyes and bring your awareness to the here and now. Give thanks for inner stability, strength, and all that you've just envisioned.

Root Chakra Affirmations

Affirmations are a great way to remind and refocus oneself when thought of consciously or verbally expressed. They direct our energies and awareness. Thoughts and spoken words are doorways to parallel, expanded versions of ourselves and the experiences they reflect. The practice of using affirmations daily assists us in remembering who we are, helps elevate our vibrational frequency, and builds a forward-moving and inner momentum toward positivity and upliftment.

The following affirmations are geared toward activating the root chakra while shifting one into a more centered state of being where one can embody the strength of spirit. They can be expressed once daily or whenever one is feeling off balance.

- I am rooted in the strength of my inner being.
- I am safe and secure now and always.
- I am anchored in the present moment.
- My basic needs are always met.
- I am fearless and courageous.
- I can navigate life confidently.
- I am trusting the process because I am divinely guided.
- I live in a world that reflects my peace and safety.
- I am self-responsible and manifesting my destiny.
- I am stable in mind, body, and spirit.
- I am abundant in all ways.
- My foundation is laid for my highest timeline.

FOUR
Sacral Chakra: *A Return to Playfulness*

Just as we have a consciousness of our own, so too do our chakras. They have their own innate intelligence and wisdom just as we do. Just as we express ourselves out of the spiritual realm into physical reality, so too do our chakras express themselves through us. We all have a deep desire, whether we are fully aware of it or not, to realize our highest potential, and so do our chakras.

Every part of us has awareness—divine intelligence encoded—from our atoms to our cells and all the space in between, including our energy centers. With that being said, the sacral chakra has an important message to share and it's this: let go of all the seriousness and stop taking everything so personal. What the sacral chakra is getting at is that life doesn't need to be stagnant, overwhelming, or a struggle. Through awareness and clarity, it can become a joyful, creative process, one of ease and flow by identifying and aligning with your spiritual nature.

Playfulness is a natural expression of the sacral chakra, and as children we were in tune with it. We knew how to play and could make up games in the moment because we hadn't yet accumulated the inner barriers that separate us from our creativeness and not-so-serious side. Our second chakra is always calling us back to our playful nature and the lighter side of life because it brings a spirit of creativity and adventure. This divinely intelligent energy wheel is our creative center, and being in alignment with it allows inspiration and creativity to express unrestricted and without struggle.

As we energize this chakra with awareness, we give it permission to activate and come online fully, leading us to experience much less inner resistance and conflict. In doing so, we shift into a version of ourselves, one with an optimally functioning sacral chakra that is in alignment with our desires and passions. In this state of being, answers to questions arrive incredibly quickly. You're able to navigate life more efficiently with less energy expenditure, and things like opportunities seem to fall into your lap because you're in a vibration of flow and allowing.

The water element that represents the sacral chakra reminds us to stop trying to swim upstream and trust the process. Being adaptive and cultivating flexibility connects us more fully with this chakra, which allows us to easily adapt to change. Let's now look at ways to connect deeper with the sacral chakra and the signs that tell if it's being activated and opening.

Five Ways to Connect Deeper with the Sacral Chakra

- Embody a spirit of lightheartedness by finding humor in everyday situations.
- Discover your passions and nurture your creativity.

- Cultivate adaptability; it will serve you in times of change.
- Embrace your sensuality by recognizing it.
- Allow yourself to have fun and pleasure.

Signs You're Activating and Opening the Sacral Chakra

- You're becoming more playful in nature, as you take life less seriously.
- You're tuning in to inspiration and experiencing new desires.
- Emotions are being understood as messengers, which allows you to experience and feel them without inner resistance.
- You're more in a flow state; experiencing greater harmony with your inner and outer worlds.
- You feel more attractive—energetically and physically—as you embrace and accept yourself more.

Shadow Work Prompts: Addressing Specific Sacral Chakra Blocks

The key to shadow work is awareness, which allows us to recognize and face self-created hindrances with greater clarity. We can only change that which we become aware of. Awareness is backed by the Presence within—Source—and by looking at negativity consciously, without judgment, one can begin the process of dissolving it. Looking at negative emotions through this elevated point of view, with discernment and fearlessness, enables us to alchemize them through the power and unconditional love of our inner being. The following energetic blocks are meant to shine a spotlight on some of the main challenges we experience as humans. Because the issues are of a mental and energetic nature, they require a conscious and energetic approach. Let's begin:

Feeling Overwhelmed by Emotions

When the sacral chakra is blocked, we can experience emotional issues, which include harboring negative emotion and difficulty in expressing the way we feel. Being reactive and resistant to what we're feeling perpetuates our inner experiences that are then projected outwardly on others or our relationships. Being overwhelmed by our emotions can have us closed off and not wanting to communicate how we feel out of fear of being judged and looked at differently.

Inner Work: The first part of the inner work is to understand what emotions are: thoughts that have been energized with our vital energy—energy in motion. They're nothing to be afraid of, but instead, things we need to look at consciously. This is so the message can be received and let go, allowing healing to take place.

Emotions that keep coming up are telling us that an energy within us hasn't been looked at and processed—hasn't been alchemized. The key is to bring awareness to the thought behind the emotion and address what needs to be possibly forgiven and released. Be mindful that not every emotion will necessarily have a message—some are just trapped energy. Reacting to negative emotion contracts our energy and traps it within us so the conscious action that's called for is releasing—as in dropping your shoulders, taking a breath, and just being present with the emotion. Be a space of awareness for it. Doing so allows the energy to dissolve in one's field of awareness.

The practice of nonreaction is one that can be mastered; being calm and relaxed even amidst uncomfortable feelings can become second nature with consistent application of inner awareness. By becoming more comfortable with our emotions through understanding and awareness, we can shift through confusion and fear and become more authentic and confident communicators.

Matters of the heart are often personal and highly charged. If one's heart has been broken in the past or if there's a trust issue at play, realize that it's not the person you're currently with that's the issue, but rather the fear or emotion being projected onto the new relationship. Old emotions and a new relationship equals the same old thing, in other words. Tending to the fear consciously by observing it, seeing our significant other through the eyes of the present and being at peace with oneself through self-acceptance are the keys to permitting the flow of universal energy to and through the sacral chakra.

Understanding what emotions are allows for some space to be created between oneself and what they're feeling, which allows for greater emotional regulation. Having greater self-understanding and awareness will invite clearer expression and the ability to share and discuss, rather than contract and close oneself off from others.

Affirmations: "I am free-flowing energy," "I am comfortable feeling emotions," and "I am in harmony with myself and others."

Fear of Intimacy

There can be many reasons that cause intimacy issues, such as past negative experience or trauma, trust or commitment issues, low self-esteem or emotional issues, for example. Experience combined with negative energy and labels create an imbalance in the second chakra, which creates issues in relationships as one closes themself off from their emotions surrounding intimacy as a way to self-protect. Ultimately, the result of blocking ourselves off from the authentic self is building walls to protect ourselves, which negatively impacts the relationship with our partner or with others. Whatever the initial cause, the two main elements at play are fear and avoidance. And with some understanding and clarity, one can address the fear of intimacy through introspection and some inner work.

Inner Work: When there are parts of us that are unhealed, we will seek unhealthy self-preservation, even in the context of relationships, through barriers, emotional distance, or avoidance of vulnerability. Because of unresolved emotions, there are those of us who are not about to readily give up the walls that have been built up because it's those very walls that convince us we're safe behind them. Identifying ourselves with the hurt and accumulated pain fuels the fear of intimacy in this case. The point here is not to diminish in any way the trauma or negative experience one has gone through, but to reveal that one doesn't have to relive the event repeatedly. Understanding that the cycle is being perpetuated mentally, through images and emotions, is the road map for undoing it and moving past it.

It's important to emphasize that one must be ready to release this kind of energy because of its very nature. We can't let go of anything unless we're ready to begin the healing process. The decision to heal the fear of intimacy begins with bringing one's awareness to the thought or emotion that is being replayed in the mind. We must remember that the thought or emotion is calling for our attention so it can be faced and released through mindfulness practices. It's important to mention that having an awareness that healing is needed starts the process of releasing; if a lot of momentum has been built up surrounding the pain or fear, it will take some time to completely take back one's energy, which will eventually neutralize the negative thought or emotion. You can come into a space of such peace and clarity that what was once the source of you feeling uncomfortable, reactive, or avoidant becomes a blip—a reminder to let go.

You can introduce forgiveness, which can be extended to another or even yourself for holding on to the fear. Forgiveness, when backed by desire and the willingness to let go, has the potential and power to shift you beyond the past and into the present—into a renewed version of you. Another tool you can apply is mental imagery, where you see yourself placing the phrase "fear of intimacy" or the negative image or emotion into a crate, closing the lid and letting it go. This is not only symbolic but is also happening in real time when you imagine it—"as within, so without."

Emotions were not meant to be avoided or feared but understood so they can be faced and released. Approaching a negative emotion with understanding creates a safe space within ourselves and with others to share, communicate, and express ourselves intimately. Through emotional intelligence we expand our awareness and invite our energy to move more freely, which promotes chakra activation and opening.

Affirmations: "I am ease and understanding," "I am aware and in tune with my emotions as being messengers," and "I am confident in expressing my sensuality."

Fear of Change

An imbalanced sacral chakra can have us experiencing rigidness and an unwillingness to change due to suppressed emotions and the resistance that follows. Clinging to old patterns and choosing to remain where one is emotionally are signs that one is cut off from the flexibility and forward flow of an activated, open chakra. Our human conditioning is what we've grown accustomed to, as it's been the only level of consciousness we've experienced thus far. The fear of going beyond it is really rooted in the fear of loss. "Will I lose myself?" "What will things be like if I let go?" These are common questions that come up when it comes to personal transformation and change.

Inner Work: Embracing change starts with the understanding that you'll not only not lose yourself in the process but embody more of who you really are. We are designed to continuously evolve and grow. The ego was never designed to be the primary consciousness for all our life. It was always meant to be a starting point, a space from which one can ascend through the chakras into universal consciousness. The gift that comes from personal change and evolution is that you don't really lose the ego in the process, but instead, perceive it differently through expanded awareness. The ego, through personal growth, will be placed in its rightful place—it will give you preferences, offer contrast to your inner light, and serve as a reminder to reawaken as you navigate your life.

When you embrace change and let go of the emotions and fears that are no longer serving you, your authentic, eternal self is allowed to come forward and be remembered through the peace and silence it reflects. Your conscious awareness remains unchanged, but it now is primarily focused and aware of your inner being—your spiritual nature. It's your inner being that is the embodiment of flow, flexibility, and fearlessness.

The practice of nonattachment is an incredibly powerful one. Being nonattached to old emotions or limiting beliefs catapults you forward into new experiences, activating potentials and possibilities that you couldn't even dream of. It's not about losing yourself but remembering who you really are spiritually. What awaits you on the other side of the fear is a life of miracles; one where all things become possible.

Affirmations: "I am one with the forward flow of life," "I embrace change and welcome it," and "I choose to let go of what no longer serves me."

Lack of Boundaries

Lacking healthy boundaries often stems from wanting to be a people pleaser and can have a negative impact on the way we feel about ourselves. When we lack boundaries, we often put others' wants and needs before our own. This is not to say that one should only think of themself—no—this is about us having the self-worth to decide with whom and to what extent we share a part of ourselves with, be it friends, family, coworkers, or a potential partner. The clarity and realization that comes from inner work is that you're responsible for your own happiness, not anyone else's.

Inner Work: Boundary work involves the cultivation of discernment and self-love practices. Being discerning starts with being in touch with your feelings and emotions. Understanding that they are a part of your inner guidance system, these energetic messengers assist you in navigating your daily life through the decision process. Your feelings are intuitive hits that are created by your very own consciousness, which is always connected to divine intelligence. All minds are joined through the field, and nothing is really hidden there.

Practicing being in touch with your emotions through introspection and being conscious of how the body feels will allow for greater clarity and the discernment that follows. In this sense, as you become more in tune with your inner guidance system by knowing there's always a message, you'll be able to read other people's intentions with greater clarity, which will assist you in creating healthy boundaries.

Your inner world, which is your vibrational frequency, is your responsibility. Because of that, you get to determine whom you share your energy and time with. A large part of a self-love practice is having healthy boundaries, which means not everyone will or should have access to you. It's this self-centered approach, not one of ego but one of energy conservation, that will pay dividends in terms of your peace and happiness. We humans have a natural tendency to put others' happiness before our own because it's something we've observed along the way. Remembering your self-worth, the importance of maintaining your well-being, and that happiness is an inside job will remind you to maintain clear lines. In essence, it's a balancing act of knowing when to say yes and when to say no through clear communication.

Affirmations: "I practice healthy boundaries," "I honor my emotions by heeding my inner guidance system," and "I am aware of my feelings as navigation tools."

Guilt and Shame Issues

As children, we are like energetic sponges. We absorb the energies, thoughts, ideas, and even beliefs, to some degree, from those around us and from the overall collective of humanity. These outer influences also include religious doctrine. For many religions, premarital sex is considered a sin and taboo, for example. The inner conflict that is experienced due to religious doctrine can have, on a subconscious level, one attach shame and guilt to one's sexuality and personal decisions. Allowed to go unhealed, the shame and guilt that we experience as children when we were scolded by our parents or embarrassed from an experience or a situation, for example, will carry on in our relationships with others, as our view of self changes due to the accumulation of these negative emotions.

Inner Work: The first thing to become aware of is that guilt and shame are incredibly low-vibrating energies stemming from what others have told us or what we've told ourselves. These dark energies not only serve as contrast to our light but also are reminders to awaken to the renewing and higher-vibrating energies of the present moment. Self-forgiveness can serve as a powerful healing tool if one has been experiencing these limiting energies.

Becoming aware of the beliefs we've picked up along the way, which includes what religion has told us and choosing to let the past go, starts the process of letting these energies dissolve. This inner subtraction of limiting beliefs allows for new, more light-filled energies to come to life. Sex is not a sin, but sacred. Viewing sex through an elevated point of view, sex is understood to be an exchange of sexual energy. Coming from this vantage point, one is discerning about whom they decide to share their energy with. Letting go of the guilt/shame surrounding sex allows it to become a holy experience—one free of negativity. Realizing that we're never being judged by Source, but rather it's us who place labels and judgments on things in our lives, we can choose to release self-judgment and shift into a more self-loving and accepting space.

It's also important to be mindful and aware that the accumulation of negative emotions and limiting beliefs and ideas are all a part of the human experience. We all signed up for this experience, and understanding this shifts us from being a victim to being a conscious participant. We chose the challenges and limitations that are placed upon us to a certain degree and the purpose in that is so we can grow and evolve. We chose to experience control systems such as religion because without a starting point, we would have nothing to leap from. Nothing is being done to us, but rather for us.

The manifested world is your consciousness pushed out, and all that's within it is designed to give you the contrast and challenges to have you look within and remember who you are beyond your humanness. This is not to diminish your humanity but to enhance it. With this expanded point of view, you can see the world in a whole new way—not as something that is against you, but as something serving you in your awakening process.

Affirmations: "My sexuality is sacred, and I honor it," "I am guiltless and sinless," and "I am attractive and magnetic."

Lack of Creativity

When one is overwhelmed with emotion, that inner turbulence can become a distraction that cuts one off from their creative side. Negative emotions are often draining, and if we're feeling depleted and defeated, we're left with little creative energy to express ourselves. Self-doubt is a form of fear—the fear of failure. It can stop an idea or a moment of inspiration in its tracks if not consciously managed. Allowed to go unchecked, negative emotion can suppress our desire and ability to create and share our gifts with the world.

Inner Work: An activated and open sacral chakra represents our creative center where we bring our inspirations and ideas to life through creative expression. To align with your creative chakra more fully, you must come back to center and the quietness of your inner being so that inspiration can be recognized and acted upon. Spending a few minutes a day recharging yourself through meditation or by taking a walk in nature can be renewing and incredibly restorative. Remembering that creativity is a natural part of you, and that being creative doesn't require struggle, can shift you into a clearer and calmer version of yourself, one that is more receptive to divine inspiration.

To get the creative juices flowing, take a few minutes and reflect on the things you're passionate about. What we give energy to expands, and focusing on a particular topic or idea will allow more of the same to come to life through awareness. Awareness and attention have a momentum-building effect that allows similar energies to come to life when you add desire and passion to the mix. Your passions are the key—the road map to creatively expressing yourself.

To manage self-doubt and the fear of failure, you must remember what purpose fear serves, which is to shake us up from our slumber so we can ascend in consciousness. Fear is contracting and suppressing by nature—its goal is to keep you from expanding and expressing your potential. When confronted with these lower-vibrating energies, you have a choice to fall for their tactics or rise above them. You are creating your own personal reality by what you believe in and what you believe is possible.

From an elevated point of view, there is no failure—only the process of discovering what works and what doesn't. Sometimes one must "fail" or experience many closed doors before the right door opens and leads to success. Failure and the fear of it is a state of mind, but it's one that can be transcended by deciding you will succeed and that you have gifts to express and share with others.

Affirmations: "I am in tune with my creativity," "I express my passions," and "I am creative by nature."

Remembering Playfulness

Life comes with challenges, obligations, and experiences that can make our day-to-day tasks seem daunting when approached through a serious lens. A limited perspective and edginess are part of the human experience because the focus is often on how difficult things are. A brighter and more cheerful outlook is available and begins with a conscious choice to embody lighter states of being. The inclusion of playfulness will not only welcome relief but also positive feelings about your life and where it's headed.

When discussing spiritual attributes, including playfulness, remembrance is everything. Remembering brings you back to yourself, gathering your attention as it reminds you what's important. Daily reflection on your inner being and its emanations is energizing and invites higher-vibrating and feel-good energies.

Getting caught up in life pulls us away from the simplicity of our inner being and is at the root of our forgetfulness. It's what causes us to be closed off from our purpose and our gentler side. The process of reawakening throughout the day consists mostly of bringing your awareness back to the peace, joy, and higher frequencies of your inner being. Shifting inward toward spirit and its love enables you to embody lightheartedness and the playfulness of the soul. I'm now going to offer you some tips on how to remember your spiritual nature, including playfulness, as you navigate daily life.

Cultivate Appreciation for Who You Are Spiritually

Recognizing the value of your spiritual nature and what it can do for you in terms of well-being and manifesting the life you desire will assist you in building positive momentum. Being in the space of appreciation attracts more like energies, thoughts, and states of being that will remind you throughout the day of who you are. With that, the playfulness will soothe the seriousness that sometimes comes with life.

Remember to Smile More Often

There are many positive benefits that come from smiling, including an elevated mood, the release of endorphins, and feelings of happiness. Everything about us is creative, including the way we feel, our posture, and the gesture of smiling. How we carry ourselves and what we extend to others reflects our inner world. Remembering to smile lightens our mood and just feels good. Making it a practice to smile more softens our edges and allows lighter energies to be experienced.

Make Time to Be Active and Creative

Participating in various activities including sports, hobbies, and the things you're passionate about will allow you to enjoy life more fully as you engage your playful side. We are multidimensional beings, and remembering to have fun, let loose, and enjoy what life has to offer will have us feeling fulfilled in the process. In performing such activities, you will naturally engage playfulness and other mood-elevating energies.

Practice Being One in Mind, Body, and Soul

Every moment can be made a meditation when you live through spiritual awareness on a moment-by-moment basis. In remembering the stillness within, you automatically unite mind and body in the process, and through that, you extend the presence of your inner being in all that you do. This conscious, inner action makes every moment whole or holy.

As you embody your spiritual nature through awareness, you rise above the fears and worries of the conditioned mind, allowing direct experience of the attributes of spirit. This state of being is not in any way bypassing or avoiding fear or negativity but rather a recognition of the futility in operating through lower and more dense energies as you remember the self-empowerment of being whole and complete. It's through your wholeness that you can navigate through life more confidently, fearlessly, and with the lightheartedness of spirit.

Sacral Chakra Healing Meditation

This is going to be a very light and playful meditation with the intention to allow you to soften your edges, let go of the seriousness, and embody a higher-vibrating version of yourself through an activated and open sacral chakra. By remembering some key spiritual concepts, such as the true nature of the ego relative to your spirituality and that the manifested world is not concrete but a reflection of your inner world, one is reminded to be an active, conscious participant in one's life, not a victim to it.

You can refer to this meditation on a weekly basis or as needed whenever you feel you need to lighten up and come back to the playfulness and joy of your inner being. This meditation should only take five to ten minutes. Let's start.

You'll need to be in a quiet space and get comfortable—sitting or lying down is fine. Close your eyes, take a few deep breaths, and drop your shoulders. Smile as you're about to begin and maintain a slight smile during the entire meditation.

Imagine yourself sitting in the middle of a beautiful park. You're feeling happy, joyful, and playful, as you see yourself with eyes closed and a big smile on your face. As you're holding this image in your mind, begin to see a circular, orange, and very beautiful energy emanate from your sacral chakra area, just below your navel. See it expanding from your being to the point where it's surrounding you.

For the next four or five minutes, see the following words emanating from the orange circle of energy—see them swirling around you as you feel love and playfulness surround you: *activated sacral chakra, playfulness, joy, creative, healing, sensual, passion, ease, flow.* As you see these images in your mind, feel the gratitude of knowing that these are expressions of your inner being—that they're being activated now. Feel the energy behind every word that's swirling around you and know that they are high-vibrating, healing, and coming from spirit.

Take a few deep breaths and then let go of the image after you've focused on it for a few minutes and affirm the following through the spoken word: "I am creative and playful by nature. I am gentleness and ease. I am free-flowing energy."

The meditation is now complete. Open your eyes, take another deep breath, and let the moment go. Give thanks for activation and healing.

General Sacral Chakra Healing

The wonderful thing about one's personal evolution and healing journey is that desire creates intention which leads to fulfillment sooner or later with consistency of inner and outer action. As you work with the sacral chakra through awareness of what it represents and what its potentials are, fears and hidden traumas or negative past experiences will begin to surface. They are nothing to be afraid of. As you cultivate mindfulness and practice being centered and awake, the clarity and high-vibrating energies of wakefulness will cause long-held negativity and limiting beliefs to come before the light of your conscious mind so they can be addressed and transmuted through various practices.

You don't have to spend a lot of time trying to figure out what specifically has been blocking your creativity or playfulness—this will only create frustration. Healing is a process and cannot be rushed. Everything unfolds and is revealed in divine timing. It's when you're most relaxed about something, in a nonresistant state, that insight and solutions can come more easily and without delay.

Five Ways to Allow Sacral Chakra Healing

- Remember to be gentle with yourself. We're often our own worst critic, and that's because of not having cultivated the deep awareness that life is a process of learning and remembering. Life is experience, and to learn, understand, and evolve, we must be exposed to what works and what doesn't. What I'm trying to get across is that our missteps or mistakes are not representative of who we are but of what we chose from our level of awareness at the time. We're not the same person we were a minute ago, let alone the person from a year ago or longer. Understanding that there is perfection in the process—even in the muck of emotions—allows us to see ourselves with compassion and grace, rather than judgment and self-loathing.
- Creativity reflects your inner being. The more you consciously embody your inner being through lightheartedness, laughter, and joy, the more you will open up to its creative genius and inspiration. Being creative is a mind-body-soul process where the mind formulates, the physical body expresses through the appropriate avenue according to the passion, and the soul inspires. If you're called to sing, then sing. If you're called to teach, then teach. Whatever it is you're passionate about, make the decision to fulfill and express yourself by immersing yourself in it wholeheartedly—through oneness. Self-expression in this way is healing because it involves all aspects of your being—it's a multilevel approach.
- Attractiveness is a state of mind, and it goes far beyond physical appearances. Self-awareness, self-understanding,

being compassionate, having a sense of humor, and being present and authentic are attractive qualities because they are attributes of spirit. It's the ability to resonate with and embody these qualities that allows one to have beautiful, higher-vibrating thoughts—about themself and others. Recognizing who you are beyond the physical and recognizing the spiritual in others makes others feel seen. This is a magnetic state of being in which people will be drawn to you not so much for what you look like, but for what you are energetically—your elevated vibrational frequency.

- Become comfortable with your emotions and the emotions of others. Knowing what emotions are allows us to create space and relief even in their presence. By approaching emotions with awareness and clarity, we become more immune to their sting as we practice meeting them with a mental attitude of fearlessness. This approach is empowering and healing. Being centered in this way, instead of allowing emotions to sway you, aligns you spiritually and also affords you the ability to be present and an active listener for others—a safe space for others to share, without the fear of being judged. In giving this gift to others, you in turn receive it yourself.
- The practice of being nonresistant, energetically speaking, will serve you well. An activated and open sacral chakra represents flexibility and harmony. Recognizing when we're feeling resistant or experiencing inner conflict offers the opportunity to see the message and then release the energy or emotion without getting carried away by it. It's very much okay to experience moments of resistance or inner conflict—they are signals to look within, read the

message, and then let it go. Narrow perspectives are often the root cause of inner resistance, but if we broaden our scope, we can sooner or later see purpose in everything.

Easing into Your Highest Timeline

Positive and desirable external shifts have an energetic beginning within you. Easing into your highest timeline is a matter of remembering the power of flow and knowing that your highest potential is already unfolding within and without. Your conscious awareness of these two concepts and your alignment with them set forth universal forces to conspire in your favor. Because you know you're on track to manifesting your destiny, detours and problems that arise are navigated with greater ease, allowing you to maintain your focus and momentum.

Moving with life through the flow state of being open-minded and receptive enables you to pick up on the divinely orchestrated cues and opportunities that lead toward manifesting your destiny. Feeling the excitement behind the prospect of acting on an opportunity is your confirmation to move ahead with its implementation. A large part of easing into your highest timeline is having the willingness to take the seemingly small steps as you feel and imagine the desire as manifested now. Through passion and excitement, what looks like work becomes an expression of joy and harmony.

When you know something as fact, it leaves little to no room for something else to be entertained within your mind. This is the approach to have with regard to the unfolding of your inner potential and the life experiences that will reflect your evolving consciousness. Know who you want to become and what you desire to do because of that personal growth. You can look to the highest self and the attributes it emanates as a guidepost. Believe in yourself and in your potential but know that you're already on the path to self-actualization and all the extraordinary gifts that come with it. Knowing is more powerful than belief and signals to the universe that you're ready to step into the next greatest version of yourself.

Tapping into dormant potentials starts by identifying your interests and passions and working toward bringing them to life. The universe is cooperative and is a cocreator in your endeavors and will provide the right people and necessary elements all in divine timing. As you align and connect more with your spiritual self by remembering and affirming you are Spirit, you will shift closer to the ease of your inner being. The universe unfolds without rush, difficulty, or strain because it's aware of its innate power, and mirroring that in our own lives would make things progress a lot smoother.

Remembering your lighter side through deeper awareness and connection to the sacral chakra will make you feel ease about manifesting your desires, as your connection with its flowing energy will guide you toward solutions. The sacral chakra is all about flow, creativity, and joy. The more you embody and remember what it represents, the more you will be able to tap into creative energies and potentials.

Having witnessed others go through the same before us, we've come to believe on a subconscious level that struggle and worry are the status quo of life. However, there is an inner path where you are present within yourself, becoming the gatekeeper of thought. By choosing to be more discerning about your self-perception and what you think is possible, you can transform into the person capable of achieving inner and outer success. The difficulty is in remaining where one is. What awaits you on the other side of struggle is a life of flow and ease through application of these spiritual concepts and the potentials found within the chakras.

Creativity Exercise

Creative expression is a natural extension of who we are as spiritual beings. The soul is spontaneous and creative by nature, and being consciously connected with it allows us to express ourselves more fully through our passions. Sharing a part of ourselves with others through our creativity is not only rewarding but also a large part of experiencing fulfillment. The following is a fun exercise designed to explore your passions and find different ways to be creative, which will assist you in your ability to express yourself creatively.

Find a quiet space where you can concentrate undisturbed. Use a pencil/pen and paper or an electronic device. This exercise should only take about ten to fifteen minutes.

Start by taking a few moments to connect with the present moment more fully, as that's where inspiration springs forth from. This is an exercise in passion finding and expression, one of listening and paying attention to divine guidance and inspiration. Begin with the following affirmation: "Divine guidance and inspiration are received by me effortlessly."

You're going to create three columns with the following headings:

- My Passions
- How Can I Express Them?
- How Will I Offer My Products/Service?

First, spend a few minutes reflecting on your passions. What would excite you? What would be fulfilling in the process of taking on such an endeavor? Think about the things you would do if you knew they were a possibility. Here's a hint: our passions are often things that we are drawn to and in a sense come naturally to us. They are often undertakings that allow us to merge mind, body, and soul.

Next, take a few minutes and focus on ways you could express your passions. Think outside the box. Allow yourself to connect with possibility. Have your writing instrument in hand so that you can catch inspiration or a flash of genius as it arises. If you've received some insight and inspiration, give thanks. If it hasn't arrived after a few minutes, relax and let go with the knowing that inspiration will come. It's often when we're in a relaxed state, one of "not trying," that ideas can come to us more easily.

Lastly, the focus is on how you can deliver or share your passion(s) with others. Will you offer your product or services online or in person? Or both? Are there other ways you can share your offerings that no one has thought of yet? Perhaps the creation of an app? Take a few minutes and jot down any ideas.

This exercise is a process that includes being present, alert, and receptive to the inspiration, creativity, and divine guidance that's offered by the soul—one's inner being. The more often you engage in the practice of going within and listening, the more effortlessly you'll find the inspiration arrives. We all have gifts to share with the world, and it's up to us to discover, cultivate, and express them so we can ultimately be of service to others.

Sacral Chakra Affirmations

The following affirmations will serve not only as reminders but also as ways to direct your energy and awareness toward the sacral chakra, thereby energizing and activating it. Remembrance plays a large role in centering ourselves in spirit, and positive, life-affirming affirmations accomplish just that. The wonderful thing about thinking and expressing affirmations that are backed by our belief or better yet, knowing, is that they attract more like energies/thoughts, which will assist and guide us on our spiritual journey.

- I am passionate and creative.
- My energy is free flowing.
- I am in harmony with myself.
- My sexuality is sacred, and I honor it.
- I am comfortable with my emotions.
- I attract nurturing and healthy relationships.
- I express my creativity effortlessly.
- I am confident in expressing myself sexually.
- My highest timeline is manifesting with ease.
- I have healthy boundaries with others.
- My life is filled with joy, passion, and abundance.
- I am a powerful creator and manifest my reality effortlessly.

FIVE

Solar Plexus Chakra: *Personify Personal Power*

The solar plexus chakra is your personal power center, where you draw inner strength, willpower, and sense of purpose. This chakra is the energetic hub where you harness motivation and the direction to move forward, accomplish things, and manifest your reality confidently. The ego is integrated and put in its right place through this chakra; it's where anger and self-esteem issues become catalysts for personal transformation. A balanced third chakra has you feeling mentally strong, capable, confident, and ready to face any challenge that comes your way.

Being connected to the energies of the solar plexus chakra, specifically the fire element, allows us to transmute negative energies and fear within the light of our consciousness. This transformative process allows us to be reborn with every shift in energy. A large part of being consciously connected to your power center is having the awareness of your inner being, which is fearless and unmoved by the outside world. This is accomplished through silent meditation and expanded awareness where the stillness within you is more easily perceived.

There is a reclaiming of your inner power and strength when you decide you're no longer going to submit to negativity or the status quo. Knowing who you are spiritually affords you the capacity to stand in your power, centered and unmoved by things that once made you feel afraid, small, and powerless. The strength and transformative fire of the solar plexus chakra is backed by the all-consuming power of unconditional love. This chakra is purifying in nature, and it helps you to clarify your desires and intentions, setting the stage for you becoming more focused. Guiding you to recognizing your ability to express your will, your motivation is ignited, giving you permission to manifest your life consciously in a confident and determined manner.

Representing your will in energetic form, the third chakra seeks to express itself according to your highest potential. Pulling in information and desire from the spiritual realm, it knows how to execute and make things happen. Fueling your desires, it supports you in taking inspired action toward sharing your unique gifts and talents with others, being of service, and finding fulfillment through the combination of beingness and doingness.

Five Ways to Connect Deeper with the Solar Plexus Chakra

- Practice self-discipline, whether it is related to emotions or diet, for example.
- Recognize the strength and transformative potential of inner stillness.
- Realize that you have a soul purpose, which will lead you to discovering your talents.

- Cultivate your self-confidence by consciously and consistently affirming positive/desirable intentions.
- Practice invoking the power of your will through decision-making and following through with action.

Signs You're Activating and Opening the Solar Plexus Chakra

- There's a feeling of self-empowerment as you navigate daily life.
- Negativity is being transmuted through observation more consistently.
- You're feeling more centered and confident.
- You feel motivated and empowered to act toward manifesting your desires and goals.
- There's a feeling of increased vitality and renewal within you.

Shadow Work Prompts: Addressing Specific Solar Plexus Chakra Blocks

When you start doing shadow work, you may find doubt and resistance trying to enter the picture in order to sabotage your goals for healing and transformation. This is nothing to be alarmed by whatsoever when you understand it's only the egoic mind protesting inner change. Continue applying the practice of observing negativity during the process, as it will greatly serve you on your ascending journey. The following energetic blocks are meant to shine a spotlight on some of the main challenges we experience as humans. Because the issues are of a mental and energetic nature, they require a conscious and energetic approach. Let's begin:

Feeling Powerless

Being disconnected from the solar plexus chakra results in an overly sensitive and impressionable mindset. This self-learned tendency fosters feelings of being powerless and vulnerable to negativity and other people's opinions about us. This results in self-pity, where we feel things are being done to us, rather than for us. The feeling of powerlessness can also be reinforced by the idea that we can't determine our destiny. Please note that we're never punished for operating this way, but we will experience the frustration, futility, and emotional heaviness for entertaining this limiting state of being until we've decided that it's no longer working or serving us.

Inner Work: Making the shift from feeling powerless to self-empowerment begins with the realization that you can't control what others say about you, but you can control your response. Remember that people's projections reflect their perception. The question I often ask myself to go beyond a situation is: "Will this matter a year from now or five years from now?"

You are in control of manifesting your destiny and are calling it forth in every moment. Recognizing the futility in engaging in negativity allows you to maintain your inner peace and power. What's most important is the perspective you have on yourself from the vantage point of self-awareness. Being receptive to the soft, still voice of your highest self and heeding its message reminds you to see yourself as Source sees you—through the clarity of stillness.

Feeling like we can't influence and shape our lives can make us feel inadequate, reinforcing a negative self-image. The source of one's suffering and the feeling of being helpless are a result of identifying with anything other than the highest self. Remember that feelings come and go and are not facts but reflections of one's current state of mind. You have the power and will to change your mind as you desire; you just have to remember the power of focus, claim it, and express it through intention, conscious thinking, and speaking your potential into existence.

As your awareness merges with the larger part of you through the awakening process, spiritual attributes will be allowed to come to the forefront of your consciousness. This includes things such as strength, fearlessness, confidence, and the understanding that you share your will with Source. Clear self-perception reveals your vastness and interconnectedness. With this elevated awareness, woefulness becomes futile, as you find greater acceptance and harmony within yourself and all of life. From this new starting point, you can choose to set forth new intentions that will shift you into new experiences as you continue to grow in spirit.

Your inner power is reclaimed when you discover that life is *for* you and not *against* you. Life responds to what we're giving off in terms of energy. As we get over ourselves, which is the maturing process, we develop a sense of reverence toward life, understanding what a gift it is. This new perspective shifts us toward awe and wonder as we recognize the magic that encompasses our human existence.

Affirmations: "I am powerful and confident," "I manifest my reality consciously," "and I am the embodiment of strength and vitality."

Frustration

Being focused on linear time, when it comes to the manifesting process and lamenting over the time it's taking for our desires to come to fruition, results in frustration. This self-limiting energetic field is further compounded when we convince ourselves that delays are denials. Maintaining this anger-created emotion will not only block the solar plexus chakra but will also chip away at your will and motivation to see things through. It will also keep you in a repeating loop of a reality where your desires remain unfulfilled.

Inner Work: The solution to overcoming frustration is to remember the following: there is a divine timing to everything. Focusing on what's missing and what hasn't yet arrived or manifested will keep you in the experience of not having. Trust that the universe responds to our intentions. Delays are part of the process, but they don't mean we're being denied; there is only that which we're allowing to come in or not. The goal is not to be happy, fulfilled, and excited strictly when the manifestation arrives but to be those things daily—embody them now, delighting in the knowing of who you are spiritually. The key is to manifest from a space of fulfillment through beingness, rather than lack and incompleteness.

Being attached to outcomes is not only worrisome but is in and of itself a lesson teaching us to be nonattached—to let go and trust the process. There's one more thing that needs to be mentioned regarding preparation: You have to get ready. Whether it's the desired relationship, healing, or long-held dream, you must prepare for it. You must embody the very thing you desire in mind, body, and spirit.

Affirmations: "What I will for my life is what Source wills for me," "I am letting go and allowing," and "I am trusting the process and surrendering to the forward current of life."

Low Self-Esteem

This self-critical, contractive, and small-feeling energy is formed by the past, but there can be secondary causes that make one feel this way. A common example is dwelling on negative experiences, such as replaying hurtful comments in one's mind. Another example is focusing on what hasn't shown up or worked out in one's life just yet, which can have someone feeling less than. We've learned to base our self-worth on achievements, such as job titles, wealth, or superficial success because the sponsoring consciousness is surface level and shallow by nature.

When we don't know who we are spiritually, we leave ourselves open to suggestion by the outside world to dictate our value and self-worth. Failing to see the immeasurable treasure and wealth inside of us, one focuses instead on the outside to receive validation and assurance, which can often fall short.

Inner Work: A spiritual vantage point reveals that self-esteem is not tied to achievement, to what others think of you, or to your past. To arrive at this inner realization, you're going to have to connect deeper with what really matters: your relationship with spirit. The expansive part of you is boundless and beyond labels and self-judgment. The soul within (that is you) knows who it is and where it extends from—Source.

Transcendent in every way, your spiritual self doesn't resonate with lower energies but instead serves to remind you of who you really are. Directing your request toward the highest self and expressing "Please remind me who I am" can set the stage for the fulfillment of the desire. Remembering your true self-worth, living purposefully, and cultivating a positive mindset that includes self-care practices will assist you in shifting out of self-critical energies and into self-loving and nurturing ones.

Another great way to cultivate self-esteem and worth is to briefly reflect on the challenges and adversities you've surmounted so far. Realize that you're a lot stronger and more capable than you think you are. Remember to honor your path—including the past with all its turbulence—rather than criticize it. Every moment is an opportunity to reawaken and grow in consciousness. We have a choice to make: to either allow negativity to continue to dictate our self-worth or allow the highest self to remind us of our glory and magnificence by going within and listening to the small, still voice. The first often offers shame, guilt, and worthlessness, and the latter leads to honor, unconditional love, and immeasurable value.

Affirmations: "My worth is immeasurable," "I am not limited by my past," and "I am deserving of a beautiful life."

Anger and Resentment

Anger is an energy that not only disconnects us from our inner self but is also responsible for the walls that are put up in the context of relationships. When allowed to go unresolved, anger manages to project itself virtually on anything or anyone; essentially wherever attention is placed. Anger is a closing-off energy that is contractive, limiting, and energy draining. Often going hand in hand with anger is resentment. In fact, it's usually anger that plants the seed of resentment when something doesn't go as planned or when someone has disappointed us. Resentment is the result when anger has not been addressed.

Inner Work: Holding on to anger and resentment can become consuming when allowed to grow month after month and year after year. Often held in the solar plexus chakra, anger will create energetic imbalances that throw us off from our power center.

The first step in resolving anger is to recognize it. Once you've recognized there is unhealed anger within, the next step is to realize that although it may appear that the anger is projected onto someone else or a circumstance, the truth of the matter is that it's pointed right back at you because there is no separation, we're all one. You can't be angry at anything or anyone without immediately experiencing it within yourself. Even anger directed toward life itself—even Source—will be immediately returned because all of life is a mirror and life is Source expressing itself.

To begin the healing process, one must remember the releasing power of forgiveness. Being created by unconditional love, forgiveness is strength in action. It's also a sign of spiritual growth, as it takes making the conscious decision of choosing peace over inner conflict. Anyone can remain angry. But choosing to forgive is true strength, as it's an inner action that is in alignment with your inner being—the soul. Moving forward, the key is to be at peace with yourself, and that includes being at peace with Source. When you are at peace with Source, with the self, anger may be temporarily experienced but it won't be able to last long. The higher-vibrating energies of spirit created by unconditional love are all-consuming; they will dissolve any lower-vibrating energy, including anger, simply through your beingness.

You should also be mindful that anger is a messenger just like any other emotion. Not only does it tell you when you're out of alignment, but it may also serve you by highlighting who or what no longer resonates with you. Awakening is an evolutionary process, one of growth and expansion of consciousness. Not everyone is meant to remain with you on your journey, and that's okay. Sometimes we outgrow people or places, and the negative emotion of anger will often point that out. The goal is to recognize the emotion or feeling, see the message within it, and then let the energy go. Because anger is not meant to be an emotional burden but rather an indicator and mechanism for personal transformation.

Affirmations: "I am at peace with myself and the world," "As I extend forgiveness, I am set free," and "Emotions are messengers, not who I am."

Being Without Purpose and Direction

Negative life experiences can leave us with self-doubt, confusion, and a feeling of unworthiness when they're continuously focused upon and identified with. The challenges we face can also sometimes leave us feeling as if something's wrong with us, which can leave us feeling defeated. The energy of defeat can snowball if left unchecked, resulting in a lack of purpose and direction in one's life. Being in this mindset smothers the solar plexus chakra and takes out its fire—the drive and motivation to make things happen in our lives.

Inner Work: The first thing you need to understand is that negative life experiences serve as lessons—reflecting one's inner state—and as potential springboards for awakening. Our human nature causes us to forget the power of our thoughts, words, and vibrational frequency to call forth our reality. When we operate through energies of fear or scarcity, we summon experiences from a higher place to shake us up—to remind us that the energy we're operating from is not serving us.

To go one step further, nothing has any meaning except for the meaning that's placed upon it. Placing a negative connotation on a past event or circumstance energizes the experience in your mind, permitting it to remain there on a subconscious or conscious level. What should also be mentioned is that you're not what happened to you. Reliving a negative event in your mind creates an identity through attachment by reacting to the emotion it causes.

To shift past the energy of defeat that results from negativity and the lack of purpose and direction that follows, you're going to have to remember the power you have within you to let the past go. You have the power of decision to choose to let the idea of defeat go, thereby depleting it of your energy. Defeat is a changeable mindset that, with greater perspective, can become a catalyst to realizing victory. Overcoming defeat starts with believing you can shift your vibrational frequency thereby changing inner and outer experience.

Cultivating mindfulness surrounding the emotional weights and feelings that are keeping you down, including defeat, lack of purpose, and confusion, will invite clarity to arise within you. Clarity is your natural state, and the only thing that blankets it are emotions and limiting beliefs. Start seeing negativity neutrally and you will start to rise above emotions and in the process, remember your purpose, and receive direction. In the grand scheme of things, your life purpose is soul remembrance. Everything else is secondary in terms of doingness. This is not to diminish doingness or the roles you choose to play but rather it's so that you can infuse joy, happiness, and fulfillment as you do the things you do. As you remember more of your spiritual nature, you will become more aware of potential and possibility. This awareness will allow you to set course in a new direction, one that is intentional and designed to move you upward and forward.

Affirmations: "I am aware of my soul purpose," "I am one with clarity," and "I am directing my life consciously now and always."

Lack of Confidence

This limiting energy can be brought on by a variety of things, but the overall issue in this case is the focusing on perceived shortcomings. Having a lack of confidence is diminishing and can limit various facets of one's life, including relationships—intimate or otherwise. As one chakra is impeded, which in this case is the solar plexus, that energy can spill onto other energy centers, depending on where the lack of confidence is projected. For example, lacking confidence surrounding the idea of dating and romance can sabotage a relationship before it's even given a chance to get off the ground, which impacts the sacral chakra.

Inner Work: The goal here is to create positive, forward-moving momentum through positive affirmations as you practice putting fear in check. Fear is at the root of having a lack of confidence. The fear of failure is what's mainly at play, and it keeps one stuck by having the person avoid challenges or engaging in many of life's joys. You must remember that fear is an illusion, but when charged with your belief it becomes a reality in the mind. It's the unconscious behavior of reaction and projection that closes one off from potentially having a different and positive, more desirable experience. Fear can't change and it can't evolve because it's not real. You are to see it differently to move past it, through present-moment awareness, that it's only a thought—a projection that is aimed at keeping you stuck.

Developing self-confidence through the inner work of mindfulness surrounding the nature of fear and choosing empowering thoughts preemptively are two of the keys to turning a lack of self-confidence into the practice of cultivating it. Releasing the need to control outcomes and surrendering to potential and possibility by approaching life without expectation can also be quite beneficial in your confidence work. As the practice of letting go is cultivated, your spiritual nature will be allowed to rise to your awareness and, with that, the attributes it reflects such as confidence, strength, and courage. All these attributes are already within you; they just have to be allowed to bubble to the surface so they can empower you to live a life of great confidence and self-trust.

Affirmations: "I am confident and self-assured," "I am more than capable," and "I am valuable and have much to offer."

Solar Plexus Chakra Healing Meditation

The intention for this meditation is to ignite the fire of consciousness within you—to have you activate your personal power through the realization that there is only the will of Source with which you share. Fear has no will or power. It can only pretend that it has when we give it the power of our focused attention. This empowering meditation will remind you how to transmute fear and reclaim your power as you revoke the ego's hold on your consciousness. Let's start.

A quiet space is preferred. Get comfortable while sitting with your head erect and your back straight. Close your eyes, take a few deep breaths, and come into the moment. Drop your shoulders as you remind yourself there is nothing to fear, ever.

With present-moment awareness, know that what you're about to imagine in your mind is happening now—in real time.

See yourself sitting comfortably in a desirable place while your solar plexus chakra is imagined as a clockwise-spinning yellow ball of energy, almost fire-like, emanating from the core of your being. See it extending out from you about 5 or 6 feet. Focus on this image for a minute or two and then see the word *activating* coming from your power center.

Feel the power and high-vibrating energy coming from your core. Know that it's backed by the all-consuming fire of unconditional love. Remember that nothing—no fear—can withstand the power of pure consciousness. Reflect on these insights for a minute or two.

For the next minute or so, scan your mind for any fears or feelings that have been diminishing or affecting your confidence or self-esteem. Fears or feelings that may come up can include fear of failure, feeling of being less than, lack of self-confidence, worry, or simply fear. When you've recognized and gathered whatever fear or negative feeling that has come to mind, take those attachments represented as words and send them into the light emanating from your being. See them being consumed by the all-consuming power of consciousness. This should take less than a minute.

Once you've released those energies into the light, take a deep breath and give thanks for release. See the word *healed* emanate from your core. Give thanks for healing. Take another deep breath and let the image go. Open your eyes and bring your awareness back to the here and now. The meditation is now complete.

This meditation should only take eight to ten minutes. You can start by practicing this once a week initially, and then using it as needed when fear needs to be put into check. As you cultivate your willpower and practice transmuting fear through observation, you will not only feel more empowered but also have a sense of lightness as you continue to release limiting beliefs and the density of accumulated negative emotions.

General Solar Plexus Chakra Healing

At the core of your being is your individual will, and it's represented by the solar plexus chakra. Life can sometimes feel like a test—a test of will. Negative life experiences or hardships can leave us feeling defeated, diminishing our will to carry on or succeed, but know that change can happen in an instant. When you understand that life, with all its challenges, serves to awaken you—it's in that moment when clarity reveals the purpose in adversity.

Your will is shared with Source because you are one. Separation is an illusion. What Source wills for you are the following: peace, clarity, understanding, wisdom, strength, and discernment. Source desires for you to know who you are spiritually, to embody your spiritual nature, to be fearless, and to understand that all of Source is for you. When we experience inner conflict and fear it's because we've shifted out of the will of Source.

Healing the solar plexus chakra begins by understanding that fear has no will of its own nor power whatsoever without your belief because of what it is, a dream of separation. Bringing your will into alignment with that of Source is a matter of letting all the fear go, remembering to trust, and recognizing the futility in inner resistance. This inner work unties Source's hands, allowing that which you desire to come to fruition. This elevated state of being is what sponsors your will as you consciously set intentions and take the inner and outer action to impress your desires on the fertile and receptive ground of your mind.

Five Ways to Allow Solar Plexus Chakra Healing

- Be mindful that your desires are divinely inspired. The desire to experience our divine aspect is at the core of every human being. Working toward seeing your desires come to life develops perseverance and the will to succeed. Through inner reflection and contemplation of these insights, you can potentially open the door to even greater understanding, further propelling you forward in your healing journey as you activate your power center in the process.
- Practice the art of nonresistance. Being frustrated, angry, and disappointed are states of being that cut you off from your personal power and place you into victimhood. Remember that there is a divine timing to everything. Enjoy the process. Turn the tables on resistant energies by using them as stimulus for personal transformation. Practice self-forgiveness in the process, as it will release you of the past as you continue to evolve and grow.
- Be your own greatest motivator. Start the day off with gratitude and set your intentions. Continue to build positive momentum throughout the day as you think and speak from a place of power and confidence. Tend to negativity as it arises by observing and then challenging negative thinking with life-affirming thoughts.

- Cultivate self-confidence. Get out of your comfort zone and try new things. Growth never takes place when we're comfortable. Researching how to give effective speeches and trying some public speaking is not only a great way to develop communication skills but also a wonderful way to develop self-confidence.
- Be mindful of your posture while sitting or standing. Everything about us is not only creative but also communicates to others our state of being as there is a mind-body connection. When sitting remember to sit up straight. This will allow you to be more alert and attentive. Good body posture when standing includes standing straight with your shoulders back. This will have you feeling more confident and assertive while also offering nonverbal signals of strength and vitality.

Self-Empowerment for Your Highest Timeline

In awakening to your spiritual nature and all its attributes, you are empowered and equipped to move beyond the limitations of the five senses and human perception, shifting into the infinite potentials of the unified field. By bringing awareness to the gifts found in Spirit, things like clarity, discernment, strength, and willpower, you in fact bring them to life. Your attention and energy are what takes potential and pulls it down from higher dimensions so they can be tangibly experienced.

All that you require for a spiritually successful life is already within you. Your inner being is self-empowered and fully equipped with chakras that are activated, open, and light filled. This higher-dimensional version of yourself is who you are spiritually. It's unchanged by the material world and will not yield to its trappings because it is discernment personified. The psychic gifts and abilities that are found in your spiritual self are available to you now—become aware of them. They are designed to help you navigate life and come in the form of intuition, energetic nudges, instant downloads, and knowing.

Bringing awareness to the solar plexus chakra and all its potential is the key to self-empowerment and moving forward and upward in consciousness toward your dreams and destiny. As you reflect on the words in this chapter and in this book, remember to be present and aware—the soul will often speak and add to what's being presented in the form of insights when higher-vibrating spiritual concepts are focused and reflected on. Awareness is a superpower because it opens the door to possibility—it makes the impossible, possible.

As you integrate your awareness with the solar plexus chakra and begin to allow it to express itself through you as confidence, willpower, and decisiveness, you will set the stage for your further ascension in consciousness. The more you come to understand the spirit and embody it, the more receptive you'll become to greater insights and wisdom. There are no limits to consciousness nor to what you can become and evolve into—the process of spiritual awakening is continuous and ever expanding.

Self-Empowering Exercise

The purpose of this exercise is to cultivate further self-awareness as you develop greater insight into how you've been operating and feeling about yourself. Tips will also be offered to help you progress toward more empowered states. You'll need a pad of paper and a pen or a pencil or an electronic device. This exercise involves answering questions and should only take about ten minutes. There really are no right or wrong answers; it all comes down to what's currently serving your growth and what's not. You can refer to your answers in a few weeks to gauge if you've made desirable shifts in how you approach life and yourself. Let's begin.

Answer the following question in five sentences or less: What limiting beliefs are holding me back and preventing me from expressing my will to move forward in my life?

As a guide, you can look at your current self-concept and the other areas of your life that may no longer be reflecting what you desire, such as your health, finances, and relationships. By pinpointing and becoming clear where we'd like to improve, we can take steps to align with our goals.

Insights: Beliefs are only thoughts that have been repeated to the point they've become a part of how one sees themself and the world. It's important to recognize that beliefs, especially those based in limitation, often determine what goals we set for ourselves. Beliefs directly influence the trajectory of our lives because they ultimately determine whether we take forward-moving action or not. It all comes down to what we truly value for ourselves and our lives. By becoming clear on our goals, we can carve a new path based on different thoughts, words, feelings, and actions.

I want to close this part of the exercise by sharing the following, which has consistently provided motivation for myself and others. Whenever I've contemplated improving an aspect of my life, I ask myself this question: "If I don't take action now, where will I be a year from now or in five years?"

Answer the following in five words or less: Describe how you feel about yourself in terms of confidence and self-worth.

The great thing about self-reflection is that it allows energy attachments to surface that may have gone undetected, allowing them to be looked at and transmuted if they no longer represent who you are now. Having greater self-awareness is key to personal transformation and self-empowerment, as it allows us to develop strategies for personal growth.

Insights: We've learned to focus on self-imperfections, which can have us feeling less assertive, productive, and successful. Remember that you can redefine yourself anytime, and choosing differently is only an intention and thought away. If you've been questioning your self-worth, know that you can choose to see yourself differently in this instant. What you decide consciously about yourself on a consistent basis is what expands in terms of positive reinforcement. Keep in mind that your inner being knows who you are in Source and by remembering the attributes it emanates you can be reminded of your empowered, authentic self.

If you've been cultivating self-worth and self-love practices, then continue forward with your positive and ascending momentum. They will only empower you and allow you to shift with greater ease anytime you temporarily slip out of the awareness of your beautiful and wondrous spiritual self.

Solar Plexus Chakra Affirmations

The following empowering and forward-moving statements are designed to assist you in directing your energy and awareness toward the positive. It's always best to be preemptive when it comes to affirmations, to think and express them often throughout the day as they build momentum as you embody them. They can also be used whenever a negative thought needs to be challenged that attempts to diminish you or impact your self-esteem.

- I am aligned with my soul purpose.
- I am strength and courage.
- My will and the will of Source are one.
- My desires are coming to fruition.
- I am focused and decisive.
- I am more than capable.
- I embrace and acknowledge my personal power.
- I am one in mind, body, and spirit.
- I am worthy and deserving of success.
- I am a magnet for abundance and prosperity.
- I trust in my abilities to realize my dreams.
- I am already living a fulfilling life.

SIX
Heart Chakra: *Let the Love Flow*

The chakras represent your multidimensionality on an energetic level. Each one represents an aspect of consciousness and is an expression of it. The heart chakra is the center for unconditional love, compassion, forgiveness, and empathy. When activated, it allows us to directly experience self-love and acceptance without attachments or conditions as stillness, which enables us to extend it to others. Being an extension of the heart of Source, the heart chakra radiates purity throughout one's being and is the unifying factor in our wholeness.

The heart chakra is the middle energy center that connects the lower and higher chakras. The air element is formless and expansive, and it is associated with a balanced and unbridled heart chakra that connects us with the infinite—the highest self. Air is giving, free, and without limits, which is why air represents this energy center. Limiting beliefs surrounding relationships, resentments, anger, and hate are dissolved in the presence of an opened heart chakra through the universal energy of unconditional love. So powerful and consuming is this love that no fear or darkness can withstand its fire because the truth of the matter is that it has no opposites. Love is all there is—that's the realization when one is deeply connected to their inner being.

Unconditional love fosters forgiveness and extends compassion and empathy. It reveals to us the futility in harboring anger and resentment and reminds us to let go and move upward vibrationally and forward. Emanating nonattachment, unconditional love reminds us to extend forgiveness so we can release ourselves of negativity. It's what also enables us to recognize others' suffering—to see ourselves in others—which allows us to be compassionate and empathetic.

A balanced heart chakra gives us the ability to share love without conditions or fear, shifting us into higher timelines with regard to our relationships as they are approached without fear. By finding self-acceptance, we accept others as they are. This doesn't mean you allow everyone access to you; after all, this is still a world of relativity and not everyone will resonate with you. As you come to understand more of your self-worth and value, your discernment also will be cultivated in the process. You may find you no longer settle for the status quo in relationships with friends or a partner. You are free to choose the people you share your attention and time with. Your energy is your spiritual currency and is valuable, so you get to decide where to spend it.

Five Ways to Connect Deeper with the Heart Chakra

- Make self-care practices a part of your daily routine.
- Express gratitude and appreciation for the people in your life.

- Practice heart chakra–expanding affirmations.
- Cultivate compassion by being mindful that everyone experiences suffering on some level.
- Practice seeing others through the present as the spiritual beings they are.

Signs You're Activating and Opening the Heart Chakra

- You're feeling greater compassion and empathy toward others.
- Forgiveness is becoming much easier to extend to others.
- You're able to process anger and resentment much more efficiently.
- You're able to see and hear others on a deeper level.
- There's more emotional balance as unconditional love is expanding within you.

Shadow Work Prompts: Addressing Specific Heart Chakra Blocks

The decision to do the inner work and face one's shadow self is a journey that doesn't have to be undertaken alone, as you have the unwavering assistance of your highest self. Not only do we have the tools to make positive inner and outer shifts but we also have spiritual guidance from our inner being and spirit guides. By affirming that one is unconditionally loved and supported from higher realms, we open the door to divine assistance, which helps us recognize that which no longer serves us. The following energetic blocks are meant to shine a spotlight on some of the main challenges we experience as humans. Because the issues are of a mental and energetic nature, they require a conscious and energetic approach. Let's begin:

Hate

We're going to start by looking at one of the darkest of energies—hate is one that goes deeper than anger. It is often peppered with disgust and suppressed rage. It's created by a trespass or multiple trespasses that have taken anger and personalized it so much that it's embedded itself deep within oneself. Harboring this kind of energy negatively impacts virtually all aspects of one's life because of its intensity and level of darkness.

Inner Work: It's important to be mindful that there's no darkness that can last long or withstand the presence of unconditional love. Unconditional love—the essence of your inner being—doesn't acknowledge levels of intensity of negative emotions, as they are all recognized as temporary states, not defining the core self. The experience of negativity may feel real to us, but it doesn't have to remain and define who we are.

The inner work to relieve oneself of the energy of hate requires a readiness, desire, and willingness to release it. If these three elements are present, that's more than half the work. Releasing hate takes some understanding, forgiveness, imagery, and surrender. The understanding is the realization that the person who trespassed against you was filled with self-hate. When one is operating through hate, they don't think or act clearly. It's a representation of a person whose consciousness has been hijacked by negative energy. Hate, like any other negative emotion, is like a virus, jumping from one person to the next when the next person receiving it doesn't have the tools or awareness yet to manage it. We mustn't continue to blame and punish ourselves for unconsciously entertaining and permitting hate or any other negative emotion to disrupt our energy fields and lives because we were never taught how to manage our emotions.

Being ready to release the emotion, forgiveness is the next step. It can be done through thought or the spoken word. Here's an example: "I forgive and release [name of person], and I forgive and release myself of this negative energy."

For the next step of this healing process, find a quiet, comfortable space. Take a few deep breaths, drop your shoulders, and close your eyes. See yourself standing there with a crate in front of you with the lid off. Next, see the energy and the word *hate* being released from your heart chakra and your entire being. It can appear as any color; the important thing is you're seeing it being released into the crate. After seeing it leave you, which should take about a minute or less, picture the lid being placed on the crate and watch it be secured with thick chains. With a bright, shining sun overhead, see the crate lift away from you and move into the sun, being consumed by its energy. Take a few deep breaths, let the image go, open your eyes, and give thanks for release and healing.

The last part of the inner work is the practice of surrender or observation. When a lot of momentum is built up around negative emotion, there may be some remnants of it for a little while longer, even after doing the initial inner work. This is nothing to fear or worry about. The practice of surrender, which is observing negative emotion, is what will starve whatever is left of the hate and sooner or later it will be fully dissolved by the elevated vibrational frequency from which you're now operating.

Affirmations: "I am a high-vibrating being of love and light," "I am free of negative attachment," and "I let go of what no longer serves me."

Holding Grudges

The inability to absolve another is often caused by the continual embracing of negative emotion, which holds us back. When we're not wanting to forgive it's because the anger that's causing this behavior has overtaken our consciousness. The rigidity of embracing such energy is limiting and can have negative impacts on one's health, as there is no separation between the mind and the body. Trapping negative emotion in the heart chakra, the negativity in holding on to grudges impacts our ability to extend and receive love.

Inner Work: Clarity and awareness are the keys to healing and moving forward in this case. Holding on to grudges is a result of reliving a comment or an event repeatedly. The thing is, the person who did you wrong or disappointed you, that caused the anger behind the grudge, more than likely did it just that one time. But for argument's sake, let's say they disappointed you more than once, even multiple times. More than likely, the person who did or said something that was untoward has forgotten it, but being on the receiving end without developed awareness allows for the continuation of the skirmish in one's mind. What I'm pointing to is that it's no longer about what has transpired but about identifying with the emotion that energizes it, thereby continuing the loop of anger and suffering. Choosing to let things go and ultimately forgive is what will free you of its grip and allow you to get unstuck.

Affirmations: "I am attached to no-thing," "I release all feelings of resentment and allow them to be replaced with understanding," and "I am free to extend and receive love."

Unable to Trust

The issue here is simply a misplacement of trust. Our human nature often makes us feel small, vulnerable, and fragile in the context of relationships. Having trust issues closes off our heart chakra, builds emotional walls, and further cements the concept of separation in our minds. A lack of trust is also a form of self-sabotage, as it closes the door to possibly experiencing a fulfilling and long-lasting relationship.

Inner Work: The approach to resolving and shifting past trust issues is multipronged. It begins by letting go of the need to trust others and placing it within yourself and the process. Allow me to explain. Putting our trust in someone else has a certain energy about it; it's somewhat of an attachment. With that placed expectation, we set the stage for great disappointment and suffering when someone breaks it. A more conscious approach is to allow others to reveal themselves as life unfolds. The truth about anyone or anything somehow always has a way of coming to light.

Trusting your gut instincts and the process protects your heart space and develops your intuition. By operating this way, you're more elevated and centered, which allows life to speak to you more clearly. This is a shift, but it's one that maintains your vibrational frequency and tranquility. A little sidenote: Once you've cultivated a deep level of trust in yourself and the process, you're free to entertain the idea of trusting others if you're called to do so. The difference here is that the trust you'll be extending to others is more conscious-based, and not so emotionally invested based on others' behaviors.

Cultivating an awareness of the invulnerable nature of your spirit can lead to unshakable calmness and inner peace. The soul is indestructible, unmoved by fear, and eternally present-moment focused. It isn't impacted by negative emotion, nor does it accumulate it. A deeper connection with your inner being will not only renew and strengthen you but will also transform your approach to current or future relationships without the fear of getting hurt. Remember that you can't control others' behaviors, only your responses to them. Allow a potential partner to reveal to you who they are by being present with them, allow the energy to speak to you; there are insights always readily available to tell you if someone resonates with you or not.

Divorce rates have been around the 50 percent mark for several years. What that tells us is that for many, the current approach to relationships is not working. Placing our happiness, trust, or any other expectation on an energetic level in someone else's hands sets us up to have that very attachment possibly backfire, robbing us of our happiness while uneasiness is created in the process. This doesn't mean that conversations can't be had on healthy boundaries within the context of the relationship but ultimately one must remember just what kind of snare attachment is.

Affirmations: "I trust myself and the process," "I am strong and centered," and "I approach relationships as my authentic self."

Feelings of Loneliness

These feelings stem from a lack of awareness of one's ever-present, innermost self. Loneliness is a result of feeling incomplete, which is a result of being disconnected from the larger part of you. Some of our natural tendencies are to seek outward validation and compare, which reminds us of things we're lacking, which in this case, could be a partner or friends. This way of thinking is what also contributes to the fear of missing out.

Inner Work: The cultivation of self-awareness is called for here, as it will remind us that one can be alone but doesn't have to necessarily be lonely. The joy, completeness, and happiness that emanates from your inner being elevates you beyond sadness, comparison, and seeking outward validation. That doesn't mean you can't have the desire to share your life with someone else if you're currently alone, but know that the energy behind it is different; it comes from an elevated awareness of wholeness rather than one of lack and wanting.

In remembering that you are mind, body, and spirit, with emphasis being on spirit, you can be led to making a deeper connection with your inner being that can be healing and uplifting. Being spiritually minded invites incredibly high-vibrating energies and feelings to express spontaneously. In the process, they comfort us, reminding us that we're not only never alone but also unconditionally loved, supported, and guided. By elevating our vibrational frequency through awareness, we rise above loneliness and come to experience the profound love found in wholeness, which lights us up from within.

Affirmations: "I am unconditionally supported and loved," "I am one with the highest self and never alone," and "I am whole and reflect joy and happiness."

Past Heartbreak

From a spiritual perspective, the issue with falling in love is that you fall in consciousness in the process. Tying most if not all your worth, happiness, and sense of self into a relationship calls forth the experiences to wake you up from the slumber of the unconscious relationship. This relationship often suffers from and is based in attachments and unexpressed boundaries. We undergo experiences such as this so we can ultimately remember the most important relationship one could ever have: the one with the highest self. When we're operating from attachment of any kind, we set ourselves up for eventual disappointment. This includes the emotional pain of heartbreak, which if left unhealed, will result in a continued blocked heart chakra and the same experiences in new relationships.

Inner Work: Unconditional love is what you are at your core and who you are in essence. It's free of expectation and attachments because the love of spirit is already complete and whole. Forgetfulness of who one really is results in the fear and fragility that often surrounds relationships. Unconditional love seeks to give freely and extend itself without expectation. Conversely, human nature often predisposes us to take things for granted and to prioritize one's needs over another. These are conflicting energies and because of the thrilling and addictive energies that arise from an unconscious relationship, we often identify with the latter. Seeking fulfillment and completeness in someone else leads to sadness, grief, and disappointment when they're no longer around.

The spiritual solution in this case is to recognize when one is falling in consciousness by paying close attention to the energies that begin to rise. The point is not to avoid the feelings that often accompany being in a romantic relationship but to feel them and experience them. The trick is not to become them. Practicing silent meditation on stillness and cultivating self-responsibility and happiness will equip you with the tools and maturity to approach relationships consciously. Becoming aware of triggers and attachments as they arise will allow you to process and transmute them, rather than paint them unto another. A self-responsibility practice includes remembering often that you are responsible for the way you feel. The more consistently you practice releasing old, stale energies and limiting beliefs that no longer serve you surrounding relationships, the closer you will align with your authentic self, who is fearless, shares of itself freely, and is strength personified.

Affirmations: "I am unconditional love in essence," "I am an extension of the greatest love, and I extend the same to others," and "I see others as they are through the clarity of the present moment."

Lack of Empathy

A lack of empathy could include many factors such as continued stress (being emotionally overwhelmed), feeling separate from others, or focusing on what's missing in one's life. The energy behind feeling unempathetic ultimately is a lack of passion for life. In the absence of the soul's life-affirming attributes, such as joy, gratitude, and peace, the result is an energy that is depressed and void of self-love and interest in life. Believing one has nothing to give or extend, one is closed off from feeling for others.

Inner Work: The first step is to recognize that this life-depleting energy is not who we are but what we're feeling. Having a lack of interest in others and their well-being reflects a lack of self-care. One must tend to the self first to be of service to others. This includes going within and recognizing the thoughts and emotions that have been entertained and allowed to dictate how one feels. This takes courage, and I want to remind you to look within fearlessly because nothing can harm you without your permission or reaction. See what's no longer serving you and choose new thoughts, new feelings, and a new outlook through the present. The past does not have to be repeated and a new life—a renewed you—is only a decision away.

Beyond the inner work, engaging in community service and volunteering a few hours a week can be transformative and fulfilling. Contemplate taking a class, such as yoga or an activity you're drawn to, so that self-expression can be cultivated, enabling you to reconnect with lighter energies. Personal growth is a process, and being overwhelmed and closed off is part of it sometimes. The key is to remember that it's all temporary and temporal—you get to decide when you've had your fill of a particular energy or feeling, when it's served its purpose so you can grow and evolve from it.

Affirmations: "I allow myself to feel my emotions without fear of them," "I am a safe space for others to share," and "I have a renewed passion and love for life and others."

Heart Chakra Healing Meditation

Activating and opening the heart chakra through awareness and imagery is the intention behind this meditation. Negative energy and emotion block any chakra. Intention, focused awareness, imagery, and surrender are the inner actions that undo accumulated negativity. When using any healing modality or approach, it's best to let go of outcomes, including how and when healing will take place. Leave the desire fulfilled to divine timing, trusting that it's already done on an energetic level.

Find a quiet and comfortable area where you can meditate without disturbance. Sitting or lying down is fine, just as long as you're in a relaxed position. Bring your awareness to the present moment as you close your eyes and take three or four deep breaths. Drop your shoulders and relax deeper into the moment.

Next, bring gentle awareness to the heart chakra in the center of your chest. Begin by bringing feelings of gratitude, appreciation, and joy to your heart center and extend these powerful and healing energies there for the next two minutes.

Now you're going to imagine the words *activated* followed by *opened* as you envision the most beautiful green energy flow from your heart chakra. Imagine the energy moving in a clockwise fashion as it extends from your being. Feel the energy expanding and elevating you. Maintain this for two minutes then let the image go.

Finish the meditation off by affirming the following statements three times each through the spoken word gently but with conviction: "My heart chakra is activated and opened. I am heart centered. I am unconditional love."

Take a few deep breaths and bring your awareness back to your surroundings. Open your eyes. Give thanks for activation and healing. The meditation is complete. This meditation should only take five to eight minutes and can be practiced once weekly for the first three or four weeks. After that, use as needed when there are feelings of heaviness or after extending forgiveness to further raise your vibrational frequency.

General Heart Chakra Healing

Playing a pivotal role in balancing negative energies, the heart chakra directs the outpouring of unconditional love throughout your entire being. Being the center chakra, it connects the lower and upper chakras—connecting the physical realm with the spiritual. Your inner being houses the subtle body, which contains already activated and open chakras—including the heart chakra. At your deepest level—in a spiritual superposition—is a light-filled and unconditional love-extending being who embodies and emanates gratitude, joy, compassion, and peace. While it is always ready to extend forgiveness, it realizes it's truly not necessary through its expanded awareness of oneness and its deep understanding of the true nature of physical reality—the soul knows life is spiritual in nature.

By embodying the attributes of the heart chakra through mindfulness, you shift toward greater alignment with your inner being. As a result, you reflect its energetic state, which includes an activated and opened heart chakra. We are energetic beings, and what we become is a result of what we're focused and aware of in any given moment. Being who we are in nature, unconditional love shifts us past the inner conflict, fear, and turmoil. By personifying the love of spirit, we allow the unrestricted expression of universal energy to restore, renew, and remind us of our wholeness. The way to access this state of being is to be centered and internally focused, including a deep awareness of what the love of Source emanates.

Soul awareness is the key to activating and healing the heart chakra, and it is the same awareness that allows continuous rebirth into the spiritual realm surrounding us. It's the soul-ution to the problem of misunderstanding one's purpose in life, the secret to maintaining inner balance, and the answer to understanding one's heart and the heart of others. Coming into conscious contact with stillness provides a doorway to your enlightened, whole, and complete heart-centered self, as it is the healing dimension of unconditional love.

Five Ways to Allow Heart Chakra Healing

- Understand the healing and releasing power of forgiveness. Forgiveness not only releases us of negative and life-draining emotions, such as anger and hate, but there is also another upshot to it: it releases us of the past. When you approach and use the timeline-shifting potential of forgiveness and extend it to yourself and all those who have trespassed you, you will find that what you do in the unseen world reverses your past errors. That's the healing potential and power in forgiveness. It wipes the slate clean. It resets and renews your mind because of its ability to cast out guilt, anger, hate, and resentment, freeing you of the chains of the past when you extend it with an earnest heart.
- Practice kindness and compassion regularly. The truth is that there are no small gestures and there's nothing small about you. The energy you extend outward into the universe through acts of kindness and compassion reaches its farthest corners. And it returns to you as feelings of love, warmth, and joy. There is no greater remedy to a heart and mind than someone who decides to embody unconditional love; it is truly renewing and rewarding on levels one cannot even begin to imagine.
- Listen to your heart, as it has a consciousness of its own. Every part of you is conscious, aware, and teeming

with divine intelligence. Going within and asking the heart "What do you require of me?" can open the door to divine guidance that can lead to personal growth, expansion of consciousness, and healing when we listen and take heed of the wisdom being extended to us.

- Add a two-minute breathwork practice to your daily routine. The air element represents the heart chakra, and we can connect with it and our life force energy more deeply through deep breathing. There are various deep-breathing techniques, and finding the right one can help you relax and reduce stress while a deeper sense of well-being is cultivated in the process.
- Practice being gentle and forgiving toward yourself. Our human conditioning often leads us to being self-critical and judgmental of ourselves. Cultivating a practice of thinking and speaking self-love affirmations balances out negative self-talk while also assisting us in healing and opening a blocked heart chakra. Being able to forgive ourselves reminds us of our self-worth and offers us relief from the emotional burdens we often carry as energetic beings. Affirmations such as "I accept myself fully" and "I forgive and release myself" remind us to be gentler with ourselves and others.

Being Able to Extend and Receive Love

The development of self-care practices fosters a mutual exchange of love and kindness with those we share our lives with. Daily reminders in the form of loving and supportive self-talk and being willing to forgive oneself for a past version that wasn't as aware, expands our awareness. By putting love in action in this way, we increase our capacity to extend and receive love. Understanding is what lays the groundwork for recognizing how our conditioning has closed us off from directly experiencing and being unconditional love. It acts as a navigational tool to point you toward your inner being, who, through its very essence of clarity and wisdom, reminds you of your true, authentic nature.

In embodying your soul, you automatically unify the mind and the body. It's through the strength and centeredness of wholeness—in having all your s#it together—that you have the immense capacity to give love through your presence and acts of kindness and compassion. This also includes being able to listen to others consciously without judgment and the ability to offer insights and guidance from an elevated point of view. Unconditional love has many facets, and these are just some examples of how it can be extended through acts of service and selflessness.

For the empaths and lightworkers of the world, I have discovered that we often find it easier to give than receive love. My sense is that we realize how much energy it takes to give of oneself and so we don't necessarily seek out receiving love because of the inner volume required to contain and extend it. I want to only serve as a reminder that you are worthy of unconditional love—of receiving it—and that you are unconditional love in essence; it encompasses your entire being. It also encompasses everyone else in your life. When we lead by example, we can often inspire others to elevate and become more loving in the process because of our demonstration of it.

Remember that unconditional love has no limits because it is without form or attachments. There is nothing it cannot renew or heal. It is clarity, wisdom, understanding, peace, acceptance, freedom, giving, gentleness, and strength all at once. It is all-encompassing, and it is pure potential and power. It is the glue that holds this reality and any other dimension together. It's not an idea or a concept but reality itself and is directly experienced through inner stillness. Emanating from Source, the remembrance of stillness is your salvation, which simply means "freedom from harm," as in the self-inflicted harm caused by identifying with anything other than unconditional love.

Heart Centered for Your Highest Timeline

This spiritually advanced way of life is all about embodying your true nature and allowing the full expression of it. A heart-centered person realizes the immense importance and value of being authentic and true to themself. They recognize the futility in identifying with and harboring negative emotions, and they have cultivated an awareness of their inner being who reflects unconditional love, joy, strength, and happiness. These self-actualizing people are still able to experience and feel negative emotions but are not tethered to them—they are free. Having grown beyond the confines of the conditioned mind, they seek to be of service and improve the lives of others by demonstrating who they are in spirit.

How to Connect to Your Heart Center

Recognizing the peace and healing that comes from being centered in your heart space deepens your connection to the loving and supporting energies emanating from it. Remembering the tremendous value in letting things go and putting it into practice to release oneself of negativity is a powerful way to heal anger and resentment and reconnect you with the unconditional love residing in your heart. Being mindful of the heart's emanations, such as compassion, kindness, and understanding, brings energy to these potentials, which allows them to be felt within us and extended to others. The awareness of unconditional love within us is what gives us the ability to remain calm and centered, knowing that love truly has no opposites.

Cultivating Heart-Centeredness

Acts of kindness, such as performing a small, unexpected favor or extending compassion to others through understanding—realizing that everyone has their own personal challenges—allows us to be a friend and supportive in times of need. Discovering your softer and gentler side through inner reflection, quiet meditation, and love-created affirmations such as "I am love and gentleness" and "I am softness and flexibility" directs your mind and energies toward bringing life to these aspects of yourself.

The Profound Benefits of Being Heart Centered

The more we cultivate being heart centered, the more capacity we'll have to give and receive love in all its facets. An expansive state to embody, this unconditional love state of being is the natural state of our higher selves. The state of wholeness as it connects the lower and upper chakras, allows for the direct experience of inner peace through stillness and the clarity to understand and tune in to others' wants and needs. It forms the foundation for great leadership, as it allows you to tune in to environments and read the energy of the room. Interconnectedness is reflected by this expanded state of being, which recognizes the value of being connected and in tune with the love within.

Self-Love Building Exercise

The process of personal growth—one's healing journey—is a destructive process. It involves subtracting and dismantling negative beliefs and old, limiting energies and emotions so we can transform, heal, and grow. As important as it is to let go of and dissolve negativity, it's just as important to replace the limiting thoughts and emotions with new, life-affirming thoughts, ideas, and more expansive states of being. And that's the purpose of this exercise. It's designed to have you remember to love yourself unconditionally so that you can not only embody the next greatest version of yourself but also serve to be a light by demonstrating who and what you are: unconditional love.

Find a quiet space and get comfortable. You need nothing else but your focused awareness.

Begin by reading this message from the heart chakra to you: "Dear one, know that although you may have temporarily forgotten your true essence by having a human experience and taking on another identity, know that unconditional love has not forgotten you. Making the courageous and selfless decision to come into this reality and experience the limitations that come with being human and being of service as a light and contrast to others, was an act of unconditional love. Nothing you do can ever change who and what you are in essence. You are unconditional love, and you are loved, cherished, and supported unconditionally, now and forever. I am the center of your being and remain ready and eager to remind you of your spiritual nature, which is without limits or fear. Remember to be kind, forgiving, and gentle with yourself, for in doing so, you will have the capacity to extend the same to others. Unconditional love is what you are and if you allow it to come to the forefront of your consciousness, it will not only heal you but also transform everything you do, making even the most mundane task an expression of joy and gratitude. With great love, your heart center."

Now that you've read the message, close your eyes and take a few deep breaths as you remember that life is here and now. Drop your shoulders and relax further into the moment as you give thanks for a successful love-affirming experience.

With eyes still closed, take two or three minutes and reflect on what you've just read. Feel the intensity and energy behind the words. Allow the clarity and understanding of the message to lift and renew you as you dwell upon the words offered.

You can now open your eyes and, with gratitude and gentle conviction, express the following through the spoken word: "I am remembering who and what I am beyond the thinking mind. I am unconditional love. I am joy and bliss. My eternal self is unchanged, and my essence remains unaltered by the human experience. I am love, strength, wisdom, clarity, fearlessness, and understanding. I am all these things and more. I am remembering who I am more and more with each day."

Once the affirmations are completed, take a few deep breaths and bring your awareness back to the here and now. Give thanks for understanding and for the unconditional love that you are. This exercise should only take about five minutes, and you are free to refer to it as needed.

Heart Chakra Affirmations

It is time to work to activate and open the heart chakra by directing our energy and awareness. These love-affirming statements serve to remind us of the unconditional love and compassion within us. They are most effective when spoken with a gentle conviction, from a place of knowing. These affirmations not only promote well-being but also remind us of our self-worth as we resonate with them. Feel free to think or speak these daily.

- I am one with the unconditional love of Source.
- I recognize unconditional love in others.
- I extend and am open to receive unconditional love.
- I am worthy of unconditional love in all its forms of abundance.
- I am guided by the love and wisdom of stillness.
- I approach relationships without fear.
- I readily forgive myself and others.
- I am an expression of joy and happiness.
- Love flows freely throughout my entire being.
- I am healed and whole through unconditional love.
- I am surrounded by loving and supportive people.
- I extend compassion and understanding to myself and others.

SEVEN

Throat Chakra: *Express Your Personal Truth*

An activated and open throat chakra provides you with the clarity, confidence, and authenticity to express yourself from the expanded awareness of the highest self. Represented by the element of ether because of its emptiness and space, the fifth chakra is all about our true selves and the limitless spiritual dimension from which it exists and extends. We are each unique expressions of consciousness, and although at our core we are all unconditional love, our personal experiences and current level of awareness allow us to express and share our personal truths through this chakra.

The throat chakra is responsible for translating higher spiritual concepts and insights, authentic communication, and clarity, including the awareness to listen and be heard. It's also a powerful portal that allows us to shift through dimensions of experience through the spoken word. Developing an understanding that we are creative at every level, which includes thoughts and words, allows us to cultivate self-awareness and discernment in terms of where we focus our energy and attention.

Working in tandem with the other chakras, but specifically with the sixth and seventh chakras, the throat chakra extracts from the nothingness of the unified field, taking formlessness and converting it into form (words) as wisdom and understanding. Enabling you to be an effective communicator through present-moment awareness, the presence and awareness of spirit provides clarity, allowing you to perceive the unspoken meaning behind words, providing deeper insights amid conversations. This gift of clarity provides you with an elevated point of view, which provides you with spiritual guidance in your responses. Being able to decipher and share one's spiritual insights fearlessly is how an activated throat chakra grabs the attention of others, as the messages are not of this world but from higher dimensions.

Thoughts are reality shifting through belief, but spoken words are much more powerful and effective because they are amplified by the vibration of our voice. Spoken with conviction and inner knowing and created by awareness of the highest self, your spiritual truths and affirmations shift you immediately to more desirable energetic states. The key here is consistency to allow what is instantly called forth from a higher dimension to express itself as a new experience sooner or later.

Five Ways to Connect Deeper with the Throat Chakra

- Make it a practice to speak from your authentic self.
- Engage in activities that cultivate self-expression, such as journaling, singing, or art.
- Speak with intention by being clear as to what it is you desire to express.

- Bring awareness to the throat chakra by realizing it has a consciousness of its own.
- Use affirmations such as "I am an effective communicator" or "I express myself honestly."

Signs You're Activating and Opening the Throat Chakra

- You're becoming more effective at expressing yourself.
- Translating higher spiritual concepts is becoming easier.
- Your connections with others are further nurtured through open and honest conversations.
- You engage in conversations with greater confidence.
- You are affirming your desires fulfilled through the spoken word with clarity.

Shadow Work Prompts: Addressing Specific Throat Chakra Blocks

As one clears away limiting beliefs, fears, and old energies, space is created for the expression of more empowering and life-giving thoughts, ideas, and concepts. The soul seeks to express itself, and becoming internally clear is what opens the door for spiritual guidance, support, and authenticity to shine through. The following energetic blocks are meant to shine a spotlight on some of the main challenges we experience as humans. Because the issues are of a mental and energetic nature, they require a conscious and energetic approach. Let's begin:

Fear of Judgment

The worry over other people's reactions (the fear of rejection) is a common fear that we experience. Our human conditioning dictates that we shouldn't make waves or stand out but rather go along with the crowd and try to fit in. This limiting self-concept, when nurtured and allowed to grow through identification with it, can create a block in the fifth chakra through worry and anxiousness about how we are perceived.

Inner Work: What needs to be realized is that we cannot control others' perceptions of us. Your personal freedom and the clearing of the throat chakra begins when you stop worrying what other people think about you. Throat chakra balancing is supported by understanding that people's tendencies are to project, that it's a common human behavior. Recognizing what's most important, what you think and believe about yourself, allows your communication hub to instill greater confidence and empowerment in your voice as fear is replaced with a greater understanding of yourself and others.

Our voice is an extension of our vibrational frequency, and not everyone will resonate with it and that's very much okay. Those who recognize your worth and value will be drawn to you and listen to what you have to say. There will also be those who don't align with your words and will be repelled. This is because we are in a world of contrasting energies, ideas, and understandings. Everyone is on their own evolutionary path and is guided to what they need to hear at the right time and to where they need to be whether they realize it or not. It's never personal, but rather all about vibrational alignment.

We are all unique aspects of Source, here to offer each other the gift of contrast, which includes differing ideas and points of view. Embracing your uniqueness, expressing yourself authentically, and consciously deciding not to seek external validation are excellent ways to overcome the fear of judgment and step into a more expressive and confident version of yourself. Know that you are more than enough and that you don't need anything or anyone to validate your existence. What should also be mentioned as a final thought here is that our minds tend to amplify and make things seem bigger than they really are. Understanding this about our humanness provides the clarity to see patterns of thought from a more elevated perspective.

Affirmations: "I am a unique aspect of consciousness," "I express myself confidently," and "I am free of worry of what others think of me."

Unexpressed Emotions

Leaving things unsaid and suppressing emotions out of fear is a form of self-sabotage. Unresolved energies that haven't been given an outlet or properly processed but instead left to build can evolve into becoming resentment and anger at a later point. This can lead to sudden outbursts of anger that can leave someone else wondering what went wrong and lead to even more misunderstandings. It's a lack of honest and open communication that can lead to throat chakra suppression.

Inner Work: There are many ways to manage and deal with unexpressed feelings and emotions. The focus here will be on two approaches: the first will be recognizing what really needs to be said while respecting and honoring other people's feelings and the second will look at how to process and clear out unresolved emotions through conscious release.

The first approach entails cultivating effective communication skills through self-awareness and the understanding that we feel because we are energetic beings. As humans, we are impacted by emotion and have a desire to be heard and understood. The question to ask oneself if you're deciding whether to express yourself is this: "Is my desire to express myself based in reaction, such as anger, because there's unhealed emotion or trauma at play or is it clarity that I'm wanting?" The first part of the question is emotionally based and divisive, and the latter seeks understanding. Self-reflection such as this will allow you to sift through the emotions and assist you in expressing yourself more clearly. It will also enable you to see another's point of view through the calmer energy of self-reflection offered through cultivated awareness. Being able to pause and reflect also empowers you to make better decisions through emotional self-management.

Let's look at the second approach. If you realize you've been triggered during a conversation due to past hurts, unresolved anger, low self-esteem, or fear of loss, here's a way you can process it and move forward. Recognizing the thought as it arises, be mindful not to judge yourself in the moment. Judging yourself for feeling emotion or negativity will only compound the feelings. You are being a space of awareness, so remember to breathe calmly. When a traumatic memory is triggered, it can impact one's breathing rate as if the event were happening again. If called to, replace it with a life-affirming thought as you remain present.

Sidenote: sometimes there is a message within the triggering thought or emotion and other times it's just the ego trying to create drama; the more awareness you bring to the thinking mind, the greater the discernment around this you will develop. Practice self-forgiveness and forgiveness of another if necessary. How much momentum is behind the emotion and how adept you are at releasing negativity will determine how quickly and efficiently the emotion will be dissolved and processed in your consciousness. If the emotion attempts to linger, know that its demise is inevitable, as you've brought awareness to it, and have realized that it no longer serves you. Do not fear it, and remember that nothing can harm you without your permission. Lower states of consciousness are perpetuated with reactive behavior, and observation is what dissolves them. If it seems as simple as following a grocery list, that's because it is. It's not the application of conscious awareness that's difficult, but rather the remaining stuck.

Affirmations: "I am comfortable feeling my emotions," "I can relate to and understand others," and "I can process and dissolve negativity with great ease."

Feeling Unheard

The energy that causes this feeling can come from feeling we've been overlooked by parents or someone in authority, such as a teacher or a coach. It can take place in the context of friendship or even a partner. At the heart of it is some form of invalidation, which if allowed to go unresolved, can be replayed in one's consciousness, creating the feeling of not being heard and misunderstood. This in turn can have someone shut down, as they see the futility in expressing themself, which negatively impacts the throat chakra.

Inner Work: Let's start with some insight. A bigger picture is needed to shift out of the feeling of having been disrespected and disregarded. We must look at this issue through the clarity and impersonal vantage point of spirit. The human tendency is to personalize most everything, which results in the unconscious search for being offended, as conflict for some can be a source of excitement. On the other hand, the authentic self is transcendent of offence because of its vastness. The soul doesn't sweat the small stuff or anything for that matter. This is not to negate the feeling of being unheard but to show the differences between our human and spiritual natures.

What should also be mentioned is that we choose a variety of challenges and adversities before incarnating into this life. We choose who we will interact with, as well as the emotional, physical, relational, and financial challenges that are designed to be motivators to assist us in our personal evolution and growth. Understanding this, we can take a step back and choose not to take things so personally. Remember that someone can only give you what they already possess. To put it another way, people often overlook in others what they've not seen within themself. To top it all off, unless they've done the inner work, most people are preoccupied with things already going on in their lives, which leaves them distracted and unable to be fully present.

The solution here is multifaceted: it begins with the understanding to not take things personal. We go unheard and unseen when others cannot perceive the stillness within themselves, preventing them from recognizing it as well as other great qualities in others. This is why pardoning others is so important in this case. It sees past the trespass and uncovers the reason behind it. We've learned to operate on the surface, which prevents us from really seeing and hearing each other. Releasing the hurt of feeling unheard through understanding frees us from the suppression caused by harboring negative emotion, which in this case, impacts one's ability to communicate.

Affirmations: "I am seen and heard," "I recognize the stillness within myself and others," and "I am connected to and aware of the vastness of my inner being."

Self-Criticism

Being hard on ourselves and excessively focusing with a negative lens on past performance or the decisions that have led us to where we are creates tension and limits our ability to self-express. What causes this self-diminishing energy is the accumulation of unloving energies that have been picked up through relationships and life experience. The energy of self-criticism can impede our ability to communicate effectively through fear of being judged and even rob us of our assertiveness. It can also make it difficult for us to receive and give compliments, blocking the flow of energy in the fifth chakra.

Inner Work: A large part of healing and overcoming self-critical energies is to recognize that we've all experienced less-than-favorable outcomes and rejection at one time or another. The negative experiences or missed opportunities don't have to dictate who and what we are today. We can choose to reframe what we perceive as a past mistake and see it as a part of our path and a lesson to make better decisions moving forward. Hindsight is always twenty-twenty, and to judge a past version of ourselves over choices made and carry forth that energy is not only futile but self-limiting. You can shift out of a self-critical vibration by acknowledging a few things. You made past decisions based on your level of awareness and understanding at the time. It's time-consuming and energy-wasting to compare who you are now and what you'd choose today versus what you chose back then. Acknowledge your strengths and achievements, as they will remind you of your progress and potential to achieve.

Lastly, invite more self-accepting and loving thoughts into your field of energy moving forward by remembering your inherent worth. Your value is not based on what you achieve or don't achieve; you are worthy simply because you exist. Every part of you, including your vulnerability and weaknesses, have value because without them, we could not have the full human experience. Therefore, honor who you've been as you look forward with excitement to who you're evolving to become. Doing so will assist you in becoming more assertive and confident in your expression as you continue to grow in spirit.

Affirmations: "I am at peace with every aspect of myself," "As I speak, I call forth my desired reality," and "Everything is unfolding in divine timing."

Excessive Shyness

Our chakras respond to our vibrational frequency, our state of being, each one acting as an energetic mirror. As children, without spiritual awareness and the tools to observe our environment, we tend to accumulate much of what we hear, see, and feel in terms of energy. This often results in feelings of anxiousness, especially in social settings, which can cause someone to shut down and become shy.

Inner Work: The work that's required here is to look within and, with intention, allow the fear and limiting thoughts that are causing the shyness to come to the surface. A short five- or ten-minute silent meditation that begins with an affirmation "I am already aware and dissolving the fear that's causing shyness" gives the highest self the green light to assist one in resolving this issue. A meditation such as this can be practiced once weekly until one resolves this fear-based issue.

Sidenote: I struggled with anxiety and the depression that comes with it between my late teens and early thirties. Personally, the conventional route failed me, as medical professionals would use a surface-level approach—place me in social situations to try to make me comfortable in those settings. It never worked because the truth of the matter is that it was a deeper, internal issue that needed addressing, not an external one. I had to get to the root of the problem, which for all of us is the unconscious aspect of us. It must be recognized for what it is and put in its rightful place, rather than being that which one primarily identifies with. We shape our lives through energy and attention, and we must discern where we direct our life force.

The last thing that should be mentioned on this topic is how important one's state of being is and how embodying a more centered and impenetrable one at that, energetically speaking, will serve you. When our minds are unguarded, we are open to being energetically influenced by outside forces, such as other people's fears and anxieties. Negative energies, just like positive ones, spread and can bounce from person to person. This concept is nothing to fear but needs to be understood. When we're defenseless against other energies in social settings, we tend to react to them and even shy away, which is how social anxieties are created.

I often hear people say, "I hate crowds." If one has the desire to be comfortable in social situations, the approach is to be aware of and embody the following: realize and anchor your awareness in the present moment. It will empower you when in social settings, as fear will attempt to project into the future the moment you feel some discomfort. Being able to recognize fear as unconscious energy creates space and relief between your conscious mind and it. There are incredibly high-vibrating energies in the now, and being one with them through awareness will assist you in transmuting the negative energies within and without. By tending to your inner world of thought and energy, you will be empowered and equipped to become comfortable even amidst uncomfortable feelings, which is the beginning of the path to mastery.

Affirmations: "I am unafraid and unmoved by the outer world," "I am centered and strengthened in my inner being," and "I am unmoved and alchemize negativity with ease."

Negative Self-Talk

We're going to look at this kind of self-talk in the context of blocking our desire to express our intentions and manifest our desires. When we say to ourselves, *I just don't see how it's going to happen* or *I'm not capable of succeeding* we're not only impacting our well-being but also inviting more of the same energy into our vibrational frequency. When we allow negative self-talk to convince us that we're incapable of achieving a desire or a dream, we disconnect ourselves from the potentials within, including the throat chakra, due to energy contraction.

Inner Work: Flipping the script on a negative train of thought requires us to look at the root cause or the self-concept that's at the heart of the matter, which is often a feeling of inadequacy. To overcome feelings of being less than, one must remember that feelings aren't set in stone and don't determine where we're headed without our permission granted to them. You get to decide the validity of any feeling or energy that presents itself to you.

Seeing the end result or desired outcome in your mind's eye should excite you, not make you recoil in disillusionment. The universe always responds with a *yes*, but we must be in accord with it by maintaining a positive attitude about what we're manifesting and also about ourselves. You have to remember to think highly of yourself until so much momentum has been created it becomes automatic, not in a conceited way but in a way that's created by self-love.

Creating a feeling of excitement every morning as you get out of bed can and should be backed by the knowing that you're already on the right path to realizing your dreams. Allow that excitement and the thought of doing the things you're passionate about to give birth to positive thinking about where you're headed, including uplifting thoughts about yourself. You have creative control over how you feel about yourself and your life. And the most empowering thing about that is that you can choose thoughts and feelings you want to experience based on who you are now, not on anything else.

Affirmations: "I am in control of how I choose to feel and think," "I am more than capable through oneness," and "Desired change comes with the positive inner shifts I make."

Discovering Inner Truths

The ability to express oneself effectively and confidently are the results of developed inner awareness. There are several avenues you can take that will assist in your personal growth and development that will enable you to connect deeper with your inner being and the wisdom and insights it holds, such as reading or attending workshops. The journey inward is a rewarding one and, much like a treasure chest, the more you look and sift through, the more nuggets of gold you'll find in terms of clarity, understanding, and inner truths.

Inner truths from one point of view are pillars that form the basic structure of one's understanding in terms of who they are and how they navigate life. You can alternate the phrase *inner truths* with *inner knowings*. Some examples would be the deep understanding that life unfolds through the present moment, knowing that nothing is being done to you, but for you, and that we are all one. These are concepts that need to be reflected upon, meditated on, and decided upon, through inner work and cultivation of mindfulness.

One's inner truth will empower, guide, and assist one in not only raising but also maintaining their vibrational frequency. Inner truth is not based in belief nor caused by the thinking mind but is a set of guiding principles. It can be referred to in virtually any circumstance, inviting clarity and wisdom to bring calm and insight when needed. Sponsored by the highest self, inner truth is unchanging, faithful, and reliable.

Spiritual truths arrive as insights, can be formed by outside sources, or are a combination of both. It's your awareness of them that starts the process of reflection, which allows the higher spiritual concept to speak to you in the form of clarity or inner knowing. As a new concept is accepted, it becomes an inner truth or knowing that assists you in navigating life. The next step is the cultivation of the realized truth through awareness and the embodying of it. An unfolding process of discovery, it's not one that can be rushed. Each inner truth realized prepares you for the next, as a spiritual foundation is laid.

Understanding the following seven spiritual principles will assist you in laying a solid foundation in your spiritual work as you continue to grow and expand in consciousness. These principles will not only guide you through daily life but will also assist you in finding your inner voice—one that is confident and unafraid to express itself. Reflect on the following and accept only that which you are ready to receive.

- Life unfolds through the present moment. You can play with and identify with the mental concepts of the past and the future, but doing so does not for an instant change the eternal moment of now.
- Oneness is the reality of spirit. The experience of separation may look and seem real, but it is based on human perception. Unity consciousness is directly known, felt, and experienced through inner stillness.
- You are the cause of your effects. Positive or negative, you call forth reality. Nothing is being done to you, and you're never punished. We experience what we are—what we become.
- Your spiritual self is unaltered by the human experience. You may take on roles and play them out, but your inner being—the soul—knows who and what it is and will not yield to this world.
- Inner stillness is your true consciousness. Silent, peaceful, and teeming with potential, your true mind is one with Source, transcendent of thought and emotion.
- You are already whole and complete. Nothing must be added to you. Instead, to realize wholeness, you must recognize that you are a three-part being—one of mind, body,

and soul—with emphasis being on your spiritual nature, which is the unifying factor.

- Physical reality is spiritual in nature and is an extension of your consciousness. This is revealed through the clarity and understanding afforded through a silent mind.

Throat Chakra Healing Meditation

In this meditation, we're going to bring attention and awareness to an already activated, balanced, and open throat chakra. Within you is every potential, including an already whole and complete being that is empowered by their voice. You will be going within and connecting to your subtle body on a deeper level and the potentials that await you there. By bringing your awareness toward your spiritual nature, you will allow it to inspire you while its healing energies are activated through awareness.

Place yourself in a comfortable position in a quiet area, preferably free of distractions. You can be sitting or lying down for this meditation. The important thing is that you are relaxed and ready to shift closer toward your inner being. Remember that there is only love the deeper you go inside. There is nothing to fear.

Close your eyes and take three or four deep breaths as you relax into the moment. Drop your shoulders as you relax further, releasing any tension you may have.

If thoughts are coming and going, let them. Resist nothing. Just bring awareness to them. Remain present and calm with steady, slow breathing.

Now imagine being surrounded by the light and radiance of the subtle body. Its colors are vivid, alive, and beautiful. See your chakras as activated energy wheels, moving in a clockwise direction starting at the base and moving upward as you feel their strengths: red (grounded), orange (playful), yellow (confidence), green (compassion), blue (fearless expression), indigo (clarity), and purple (oneness). Feel the power and potential of these energy centers for the next two minutes as you are reminded that they are for you, awaiting your command as you remember that they are extensions of unconditional love.

Next, bring your attention to the throat chakra. Take a deep breath and with that, see the throat chakra become energized—vibrating and becoming a brighter blue. Know that it's being activated and that it's guided by divine intelligence.

As you exhale, see any blocks or fears being released by it in the form of words, for example: *fear*, *fear of being judged*, *self-critical*. Watch these energies dissolve as they are released in your mind's eye.

Continue this process of deep breathing—activating—releasing for the next two minutes. Once you're done, let the image go and bring your awareness back to the wholeness of you and to your subtle body. Continue to see the chakras within it activated and open, lighting up your entire being for the next minute.

Next, affirm the following through the spoken word: "I am one in mind, body, and spirit. I am connected to my subtle body and its divine intelligence. I am connected to the voice of my highest self."

Take a few deep breaths and let any images go. Open your eyes and give thanks for activation and healing. Bring your awareness to the here and now. This meditation needs only about ten minutes. Performed once, it only needs to be practiced moving forward as you're called to it.

General Throat Chakra Healing

A powerful approach to healing is to cultivate both an inner and an outer environment that embodies or represents the desired state. The key inner elements to any healing are desire, intention, allowing, and surrender. Desire starts the engine—it's what directs universal forces. Intentions are the conscious thoughts and spoken words that shift you to the desired reality. Allowing is the cultivation of mindfulness, where you practice starving doubts and inner resistance. And surrender is trusting in divine timing as you let go of how and when the desire will be fulfilled. The key outer element entails acting as if the desire is already manifested, which includes inspired actions that represent one who is whole.

Throat chakra issues can be resolved by approaching them with an awareness, such as what was just offered. Your desire to activate, open, and heal the throat chakra must begin with the desire and inner knowing that it's already accomplished or done. From that awareness, speak your desires through life-affirming and healing affirmations. Practice mindfulness as you consciously recognize and release the fears and limiting beliefs that no longer serve you as you trust the process that allows for the spontaneous expression of healing in divine timing.

Self-reflection and journaling how you'd like your voice to be heard will clarify your ability to self-express. The practice of mindful expression (choosing your words consciously) and using your voice through community engagement on the things you're passionate about are also helpful. It's this wholeness approach—mind, body, and spirit that has such reality-shifting power—that has the potential to empower and heal.

Five Ways to Allow Throat Chakra Healing

- Find your strengths and cultivate them through your voice. We all have gifts within us that are waiting to be discovered and actualized. One of the keys to discovering your strengths is to look to your passions. Another approach is to try new things. As you work on developing your strengths, remember to speak desires, intentions, and affirmations of your strengths. Doing so will assist you in directing your energy while you activate the throat chakra in the process.
- Cultivate a spirit of fearlessness. The practice of mindfulness where you are aware of the nature of fear will empower you to know when it presents itself, which will enable you to dismiss it as it arises. By consistently doing the inner work, you'll be able to extend your expanded awareness to all aspects of your life, including your voice and ability to communicate. Through self-understanding you can be comfortable not only with yourself but also with others, regardless of the setting.

- Practice positive self-talk. Negativity must be met with positivity because it shifts momentum. By choosing positive and uplifting thoughts daily, you not only cultivate inner balance but also raise your vibrational frequency. Our minds require direction, and positive self-talk is one of the ways to direct it.
- Develop your understanding of self and others. Once you have a better understanding of yourself, you can extend greater empathy toward others. Recognizing your own inner challenges and varying perspectives brings to light that everyone has their own personal set of biases and experiences that create the lens in which they see the world. With this knowledge, you're reminded to not react to other people's viewpoints. This awareness allows you to extend understanding and compassion toward yourself and others, which is not only a gift but also healing.
- Remember that your words are powerful and reality-shifting. In recognizing the power of your words, you activate the potential of the throat chakra. Everything about you is creative, as you are an extension of Source. Nothing about you is small, and there really are no small acts of expression. By understanding your ability to call forth reality, you become more discerning as to what you focus on and talk about. It's this awareness that shifts one toward speaking gratitude and appreciation, which opens the door to more things to be grateful and appreciative for.

Confident Self-Expression for Your Highest Timeline

The healing journey that so many of us embark upon entails personal growth and is the path toward enlightenment, which is a destructive process that tears down anything that is no longer serving us. Before one can become fearless, fear must be understood so we can recognize our true, authentic, spiritual self. This leads to the understanding of oneself and how life works as cause and effect and self-responsibility come front and center through self-awareness. Expressive by nature, your inner being is spontaneous and teeming with creative talents waiting to be expressed.

The key to confident self-expression is your awareness of stillness. Integrating stillness allows the certainty and confidence of spirit to be imbued with all your undertakings, creative or otherwise. The soul knows it can accomplish anything and operates from the end—it sees whatever the task is before it as already done. It's this level of confidence that's available to every one of us and its unfolding begins with awareness.

When you are operating at soul-level confidence, you are beyond belief and into the realm of knowing. It's the energy behind knowing that bypasses lower frequencies, straight toward your highest timeline. You must know who you are in Spirit—you are confident, capable, and already in alignment with your highest timeline. Confidence is backed by inner conviction that, when developed, makes a way when there doesn't seem to be one. It looks to one's intentions and elevated vibrational frequency for confirmation that success is yours.

As you make progress in your spiritual growth and evolution, you will find that the soul will express itself increasingly through nonresistance as synchronicities, inspiration, creativity, clearer divine guidance, and greater understanding. It's these expressions that, when noticed and followed through by action, will guide you in shifting into more desirable experiences as you relax in the knowing that Source is unfailing. Coming into your full potential is an unfolding process. When realized, it is one that is beyond fear, struggle, and worry. Understandably, it's contrary to what we've been conditioned to believe; as humans, we've been told directly and indirectly that struggle is a part of achieving success. But then again, the old definition of success has been based on material gain, not on self-actualization.

Communication Skills Exercise

Effective communication skills reflect self-awareness, clarity, active listening, and confidence. Operating from a vibrational frequency that has integrated personal growth practices through self-reflection provides the tools necessary to be an effective communicator. This exercise is a self-reflecting one that will give you insight into where you are and how you can move forward in further developing authentic and confident communication, which will empower you through an activated and balanced throat chakra. From start to finish, this exercise shouldn't take longer than ten minutes.

For this exercise you'll need a quiet space to concentrate, and a pen or a pencil and a pad of paper or an electronic device to jot down your answers. Be mindful that there are no right or wrong answers; it's about self-discovery and insight. Take a few minutes to reflect on each question, then jot down your answers.

First question: In ten words or less, describe how effective and authentic your communication skills currently are.

Second question: In ten words or less, describe the attributes of an authentic and effective communicator.

Once you've answered the second question, take a few minutes and compare answers between questions. Are the descriptive words similar? Are they the same? Is there a big difference between the two? Is there room for improvement? These are just questions to ask yourself as you compare answers.

Third and last question: If you have found you could benefit from some improvement in your communication skills, what inner and outer steps could you take to achieve the desired outcome? Spend a few minutes brainstorming and then jot down your answers.

The purpose of this exercise is to offer clarity through self-reflection, as it will offer direction as to what actions to take. You can refer to this exercise in three months to see how far you've come. You'd be amazed how much progress can be made in so little time with just some cultivated awareness that's been put into practice.

Throat Chakra Affirmations

When we look beyond the world of form, which includes the physical body and thoughts, we find we are enveloped by formlessness—the unified field or world of Spirit. Remembering who we really are and where we really are reminds us that we are the cause of our effects, that not only do we manifest our reality but also that we have free will. We don't have to allow the outside world to dictate our destiny; we can remember that we're empowered to consciously call forth experience. Let these affirmations remind you of the creative power you have through oneness. Feel the strength and voice of Spirit behind them as you allow them to lift you up and forward.

- My spoken intentions are heard and instantly fulfilled by Source.
- I speak all forms of abundance into existence, including clarity and understanding.
- I am empowered to manifest my desires into reality.
- My voice is powerful and expresses authentically.
- I am a confident speaker.
- I express myself with ease and am understood.
- I am safe to express myself.
- I am aware of the power of my voice.
- I am an active and conscious listener within and without.
- My voice is calming and soothing.
- I am comfortable with myself and amongst others.
- My voice is backed by the power of oneness.

EIGHT
Third Eye Chakra: *See Clearly*

The sixth chakra is the key to embodying your boundless, spiritual self. It is the doorway to divine intelligence, including being able to recognize and bring to life your psychic abilities. An activated and open third eye represents the enlightened state, which enables one to see beyond what the physical eyes perceive. With expanded awareness, you're now able to recognize the realm of Spirit surrounding you.

Providing access to the dimension of inner stillness, it's no wonder that light is the element that represents this powerful spiritual faculty. The inner light of stillness allows us to see the ego clearly, thereby dissolving it and revoking its power over our consciousness as we reclaim ourself through the remembrance offered through a silent mind.

As you embody your authentic self, clarity is allowed to express itself as inner knowing, intuition, and heightened physical senses—you're now operating beyond belief. You not only feel more but also sense more as discernment is developed through spiritual alignment. This allows you to read energy as information within and without. This ability empowers you to understand yourself on the deepest of levels of mind and spirit. Through self-understanding, you can extend the same gift to others through empathy and compassion.

With a clear mind, you access divine guidance with greater ease through the silence of your inner being. Knowing that wisdom is a one-way street, your awareness is focused on the highest self, where you are reminded of your potential and given the spiritual tools to navigate your life fearlessly and with great confidence and certainty. In transcending self-created limits, you lighten up and raise your vibrational frequency to that of Spirit—unconditional love—where no fear, worry, or doubt can last long.

When you are no longer identified with the shadow self, its hold on your consciousness is loosened. Now orbiting the surface of your mind rather than being attached to it, you are free. The primary cause of inner turmoil now becomes a contrast to your inner light of consciousness and a reminder to reawaken as it presents itself as negative thought and emotion. It's now a whisper, reminding you when you've come out of alignment—out of the safety and peace of stillness. The catalyst to your awakening, you realize the ego is the bringer of light—the necessary darkness to direct you toward the light of your inner being.

The opening of the third eye signals the end of unconscious suffering and is an act of grace, one that cannot be forced but invited through desire and a willingness to surrender to the highest self. The activation of this chakra is your sign, informing you that you've come into your highest timeline in terms of how you feel and experience life through the integration of mind, body, and spirit. As you cultivate your spiritual practice and allow for inspiration and divine guidance, you will know what actions to take and how to be of service. This will allow your renewed and transformed inner world to be a demonstration of what's possible while being a source of inspiration to others.

Five Ways to Connect Deeper with the Third Eye Chakra

- Make challenging negative thoughts a consistent practice.
- Cultivate a spirit of fearlessness by understanding the false self and how it operates.
- Remember often that what you see in the outer is a reflection of the inner.
- Practice being alert; be aware of messages that come from within and without.
- Know that the third eye is a very real spiritual faculty and is always operating at some level.

Signs You're Activating and Opening the Third Eye Chakra

- You feel vibrating/an opening feeling in the middle of your forehead at times.
- You're becoming more aware of synchronicities in your life.
- Inner stillness is being recognized and experienced as a silent mind more frequently.
- You're beginning to contemplate the deeper meaning of life.
- Psychic abilities are becoming more apparent.

Shadow Work Prompts: Addressing Specific Third Eye Chakra Blocks

There's an abundance of spiritual treasures and insights residing within you, patiently waiting for recognition. As you dig deep within yourself and uproot long-held limitations through self-healing practices, you will realize all that you've been seeking is within, not without. The following energetic blocks are meant to shine a spotlight on some of the main challenges we experience as humans. Because the issues are of a mental and energetic nature, they require a conscious and energetic approach. Let's begin:

Closed-Mindedness

Being closed off to new spiritual concepts and possibilities inhibits the third eye and can hinder the expansion of one's consciousness and psychic development. Spiritual gifts and tools are energies, potentials within you, and they require your openness and awareness to come to life. Being closed-minded is a form of resistance that promotes stagnation and can prevent one from coming into their full potential.

Inner Work: One thing to become aware of is that our latent talents and psychic gifts are already in existence, just beyond our awareness. You could say they're in a higher realm, above us, waiting to be downloaded and translated as intuition, wisdom, and much more. Openness and receptivity are crucial for directly experiencing these supporting energies, giving the universe the green light to activate and express them through you.

Closed-mindedness often stems from the core belief that life and what one has experienced thus far are all there is to it. To break free from this limiting belief, start by creating curiosity about your potential and what life really is. Begin by asking questions like:

"Is this all there is to life?" "What if there's more to human beings than just our five senses?" "If the third eye is a potential within me, what actions should I take to come into alignment with it?" I've realized in my own personal experience that when I began to ask the bigger questions around life and my own existence, the answers always arrived sooner or later. My deep desire to understand the unknown fueled my curiosity and ultimately led me to third eye activation and the expression of its potential.

Affirmations: "I am open to higher spiritual concepts and understanding," "My deeper questions to life are being answered," and "I am aware of the third eye's potential within me."

Disregarding Intuition

Our intuition serves several purposes, and one of those is to assist us in navigating life in an empowered way, thereby enabling us to manage adversities with greater ease or even transcend them altogether. But when disregarded, we instead follow our human perception, which is limited relative to our spiritual nature. Because of this, we can feel like we've taken a few steps backward, even regretting choices that were driven by fear or lack, rather than our inner knowing. Operating this way creates inner conflict while also further disconnecting us from the guidance offered by our intuition afforded through the sixth chakra due to self-doubt.

Inner Work: A two-pronged approach is needed here, and it involves first recognizing our intuition as a powerful spiritual tool that we already possess and can help guide us through life. The second part of the inner work involves honoring our intuition by cultivating it through awareness. You have come into this world lacking nothing. When you understand this by remembering your spiritual nature—the part of you that embodies clarity and divine intelligence—you will recognize the wholeness already present within. This can be further established through meditative practices and becoming aware of the synchronicities already taking place in your life. Your intuition, including all your psychic abilities, has great potential and is ready and waiting to express through you. But you first need to bring awareness to it because your directed energy to spiritual concepts is what brings it to life.

Make it a practice to bring awareness into your moments and the world around you. Life, and everyone in it, is speaking to you. Every encounter is a potential teacher and has a message to those who are aware. The wonderful thing about cultivating awareness, especially surrounding one's intuition, is that it opens the door to more of the same—creating positive momentum. Increasing awareness of the third eye and its potential boosts the possibility of a third eye activation, which would allow its insights and spiritual abilities to express freely.

Affirmations: "I am in tune with my intuition," "I honor my intuition and psychic abilities through the awareness of them," and "I make decisions through inner knowing and not fear."

Excessive Stress

When negative thinking and the emotions that follow aren't managed consciously through practices such as mindfulness, forgiveness, and trust, the result is often an accumulation of negative energy. This can be quite disruptive, causing inner conflict, tension, fear, and worry. Losing sight of what's important, our energy field grows heavy, clouded, and at the mercy of external conditions that cuts us off from the peace and understanding offered through a balanced third eye.

Inner Work: When we're exposed to stress over several months or years, it's easy to believe that it's our natural state of being—we become conditioned to it. To begin to shift out of a stress-filled state and into one that is more relaxed and peaceful, we need to remember what our true spiritual state of being involves. Realizing there are higher and more empowered states of being available provides you with a target to aim for in terms of relief. Your natural state is one of peace, clarity, trusting, and joy offered through soul awareness.

By recognizing the value and importance of embodying these higher states of being, one can make conscious choices to move toward them. This starts by first understanding that negative and stress-filled states are caused by identifying with something we're not. Alignment with anything other than our inner being leaves us open to stress-related energies because that's what's mostly found outside of stillness. Stress arises not so much from the eternal issue or problem but from our perception of it. Recognizing one's addiction to stress through self-awareness is a big step toward inner balance. All negative energy stems from attachments that are addictive by nature. Develop a spirit of gratitude and discover things outside of work that you are passionate about and find fun and fulfilling. The experience of stress calls us to remember and engage our lighter side—our spiritual nature—which is unafraid, unmoved, and empowered to see beyond the five senses.

Affirmations: "I balance negative thoughts with positive, life-affirming thoughts," "I am releasing what no longer serves me by choosing nonreaction," and "The power of consciousness within me is more than able to consume any negativity."

Lacking Clarity

Forgetting who we are and what our life's purpose is often results in the confusion one experiences when one is solely identified as a human being. We each have a creative side, hidden talents, and undiscovered abilities that require us to connect with our spiritual selves for them to fully express. Spiritual amnesia blankets our potential, which includes the third eye, from empowering and guiding us to live with knowingness, direction, and a vision for our lives.

Inner Work: As spiritual beings having a human experience in a world of relativity, we often find ourselves experiencing a particular energy that causes a certain state of mind, which creates the desire to experience its opposite. In this case, confusion must come before clarity. Understanding that we need a starting point, a level of consciousness from which to evolve, gives us some insight and understanding to the experience of lacking clarity or being confused on which way to go in life. From this vantage point of understanding the purpose behind confusion, the next step is to remember your potential and what you're capable of manifesting in your life. This inner work entails remembering you're a three-part being—mind, body, and soul. Remembering that the soul inspires, the mind sets the intentions, and the physical body is required to take action to realize the dream or desire, gives us the road map to making things happen in our life.

As you cultivate clarity and purpose through greater self-understanding and creating a vision for your life, you'll allow for greater detection of inspiration when it's presented. Inspiration is usually high-vibrating and passion-filled, and it arrives as an idea teeming with excitement. It's your job to recognize it, formulate an initial plan of execution, and then take the necessary steps. It's also vital to leave room for adjustment and approach your vision with a spirit of gratitude that recognizes that the desire or dream has already been fulfilled. In summary, remember who you are and what your purpose is, then embody the person who is clear and manifesting their destiny through a mind, body, and soul approach, which will activate and engage your spiritual faculties in the process.

Affirmations: "I know who I am and what my potentials are," "I am focused and clear," and "I am divinely guided and pay attention to the intuition that's always offered."

Overreliance on Thinking

Navigating the manifested world requires us to use logic and reason. These tools allow us to understand cause and effect, make decisions, and manage our lives. As great as logic and reason are at dissecting things, they often fall short in terms of having a greater perspective and taking into account spiritual energy and forces beyond the natural world. Overthinking hinders our ability to access the higher mind's perspective and utilize the spiritual tools we have at our disposal.

Inner Work: An activated and open third eye doesn't dissolve you of logic and reason but complements it. It ushers in balance between the lower and higher minds by bringing to life the aspect of you that uses energy, feeling, and energetic information. By introducing this spiritual perspective, we connect to intuitive insights and wisdom unavailable through logic and reason.

You can work toward integrating and activating the third eye by becoming aware that your soul communicates through stillness as feelings and inner knowing. Developing the ability to receive this spiritual communication involves actively seeking the silent spaces between thoughts. Becoming internally quiet by focusing on the concept of "nothingness" enhances one's receptivity to higher awareness. This in turn aligns you with the third eye's primary function, which is to assist you in accessing the spiritual dimension within you. Enabling you to connect to wisdom as it arrives as knowingness and supporting energies based in intuition are also part of its function. The more awareness you bring to the third eye and its potential, the more you can perceive life from a spiritual lens and develop trust in your intuition and gut feelings.

Affirmations: "I call forth my reality through awareness and intention," "I am able to access greater wisdom and intuition," and "My inspired imagination reveals what is possible."

Spiritually Disconnected

The third eye is the corridor that connects us to the highest self and universal consciousness. It's the single vision (oneness) that allows us to perceive the spiritual realm that surrounds us. It's always operating at some level, but when we lose sight of the bigger picture and perceive obstacles and challenges as punishments rather than opportunities to expand and grow, it's easy to lose faith and trust in the process. This in turn can have one feeling disappointed and frustrated, which creates energetic walls between the conscious mind and the higher self. It's this energetic separation created in the mind as resentment that can cause a rebellious attitude toward life—Source—which then compounds matters further. Descending in consciousness through negative emotion, we cut ourselves off from the understanding and spiritual vantage point offered through the third eye.

Inner Work: We begin with some clarity and insight into our forgetfulness regarding the purpose of challenges and why we showed up here in the first place. Appearing in different forms—health, relationship, financial, and emotional—challenges are designed to (a) show us how our current belief system on a particular subject is no longer serving us and (b) awaken us from the slumber of identifying with limiting thoughts. The thoughts and emotions that we entertain daily are what call forth the experiences because all of life is a mirror. We experience what we are energetically.

We all signed up for the human experience, including all the ups and downs that come with it. Before incarnating, from our spiritual vantage point, we saw the opportunity to incarnate as an adventure. Knowing that we're always one with Source, and that there's nothing we can't heal or accomplish, we projected a part of ourselves into physical reality, experiencing the density of the manifested world. In the process of taking human form, we forgot our unchanging interconnectedness with Source, and through that forgetfulness, we created a separate identity and all the branching, limiting beliefs that come from doing so.

What I'm pointing out is that the lack of faith, trust, and resentments we experience are understandable but are not backed by facts. Instead, they are created by misunderstanding and identifying with anything other than our inner being and the stillness it emanates. You and Source are one. You can forget your oneness, but it doesn't change what is.

Faith and trust are powerful forces that require cultivation, and that cultivation begins by affirming that you're not going to allow the past to be repeated but instead choose differently by deciding to have faith and trust in yourself and the process. The healing process surrounding the belief in separation and the feeling of being disconnected starts with a desire to reconnect and a willingness to forgive oneself—including Source. This entails a spirit of surrender that is the conscious releasing of the limiting beliefs, preconceived notions on how life works, and the negative emotions surrounding your relationship with Source.

Spending some time alone can really help you reconnect and shift toward the empowering state of oneness. Find a quiet space and, with desire, express the following through thought or the spoken words: "I forgive and release myself for not understanding and am letting go of the emotions that no longer serve me. I forgive Source and release any and all resentments, as they were based on misunderstanding and attachment to outcomes. I surrender what no longer serves me and choose to reconnect and remember my oneness with everything and everyone, including Source."

I wanted to wrap up this section with a few more insights on forgiveness. When practiced with desire and a willingness to let go, I have found that it's a force that can free us from guilt, sadness, shame, and negativity. Wiping the slate clean and shifting us into the renewing energies of the present, forgiveness is a powerful ally in your healing journey. Forgiveness is timeline shifting, allowing us to get unstuck and move past layers of accumulated emotions and into a more spiritually connected version of ourselves, which is operating with greater peace, insight, and understanding.

Affirmations: "I forgive myself and Source, as I did not understand the purpose in suffering," "I am connected to the highest self and my spiritual faculties now and always," and "I am aware of and embody my spiritual nature."

Integrating Spiritual Faculties

You may have noticed that as we ascend in the chakras, we come into greater potentials and understandings. This is not to say that one chakra is more important than another; for each one plays an integral part of the ascension ladder. What I'm pointing to is that the higher we ascend in consciousness, the closer we come to connecting with our inner being—Source itself—and all its potential and vastness of intelligence, understanding, wisdom, and insight.

Our spiritual faculties include but are not limited to: awareness, faith, trust, surrender, compassion, gratitude, discernment, intuition, clarity, wisdom, understanding, forgiveness, and imagination. Because they are interconnected through the dimension of inner stillness (close in frequency), each spiritual faculty or tool allows for the remembrances of the others. For example, cultivating awareness of one's intuitive nature can open the door to the expression of profound discernment and clarity. The contemplation and reflection on a particular spiritual faculty invites insight into its potential and possibilities.

Being mindful of the spiritual faculties that you already possess and putting them into practice will shift you into higher states of consciousness and the timelines that reflect them. Your inner world and awareness transport you to parallel realities based on the current vibrational frequency from which you're operating. Faculties like understanding and discernment need to be recognized for what they truly are: powerful, life-changing spiritual forces. Understanding, for example, has the power to assist you in navigating your life with greater awareness and wisdom. Discernment that's been cultivated allows you to see beyond the veil (of thought) and see and read energy—the deeper meaning behind seemingly random encounters.

The key to integrating your spiritual faculties is to embody them by expressing and extending them to others through kindness, compassion, and the awareness of oneness. In being aware of their potential and power to heal, transform our lives, and cultivate fulfillment in the process, we recognize their immense value through gratitude and appreciation that further elevates us.

Going within, listening, and paying attention are how wisdom, clarity, understanding, and many of your other spiritual faculties are directly experienced—through inner silence. Extending from the highest self, these spiritual gifts are received through a clear mind that's open and willing to know. Beyond belief or thoughts, these empowering energies arrive as vibration, feeling, and knowing. The practice of being still, silent, and alert will serve you in the development of not only these potentials but also many others.

The introduction and practice of your spiritual faculties assist you in creating inner balance, strength, resilience, and a deeper understanding of your potential. In merging spiritual awareness and the gifts found within it with your humanity, you come into balance. As one hand is grounded into your humanity, the other reaches upward toward the highest self and the vastness of consciousness that is your spiritual inheritance. Claiming it requires your recognition of it, which will unfold and progress through awareness and embodiment.

Third Eye Chakra Healing Meditation

There is great healing potential and power in the third eye. When activated, the mind becomes silent, as incredibly high-vibrating universal energy is allowed to fill your entire being, lighting you up inside. It's important to remember that its activation is based on one's readiness and willingness to transcend and go beyond the conditioned mind. Divine timing is always at play, and Source knows when you are ready. This meditation is an intention in essence; a signal to the highest self that one is ready to ascend in consciousness.

Place yourself in a comfortable position in a quiet space. Sitting up with your head straight and shoulders relaxed, come into an awareness of the present moment.

Close your eyes and take a few deep breaths. Drop your shoulders once more and relax your facial muscles as you bring your awareness to the third eye.

For the next two minutes, just be a space of awareness as you focus your attention on the area just above and between your eyebrows. You may feel some slight tingling or opening as you do this. Just continue to relax as you observe and feel.

Next, imagine the third eye activating, expressing its indigo color, and opening as an energetic eye. Envision golden white light entering from the top of your head, radiating throughout your entire being. Focus on this image for two minutes as you feel yourself getting lighter and vibrating higher.

Let the image go and then affirm the following to the third eye: "I am aware of your reality and am ready to be divinely guided in all aspects of my life. I give thanks for your activation and opening. I surrender my awakening to divine timing."

Take a few deep breaths and let the moment go as you open your eyes. Come back to the here and now.

If you feel inspired, give thanks again as you remember to let go of outcomes.

This meditation only takes about five minutes or so and needs to be only performed once. Trust that your desire is heard and received by Source. There is no mistaking a third eye activation when it occurs; at that moment, you will know. This activation signals one's upcoming ego death and is the end of one's old life of limitation, as one is reborn into the unified field and all its unlimited potential.

General Third Eye Chakra Healing

Spiritual awareness and the integration of it in daily life is a powerful way to bring to life spiritual faculties while also maintaining and even raising your vibrational frequency to states of clarity, joy, and nonattached happiness. Making the choice to embody your spirituality through self-awareness, acts of service, and practicing the art of nonattachment are ways of demonstrating one's wholeness. It's by honoring all aspects of oneself, the physical and the spiritual, that peace and harmony are cultivated, creating authentic expression of your various facets.

Expression is a powerful form of healing. It allows potential energy to release and expand, thereby unlocking hidden talents and abilities. When we express ourselves creatively, whether it be through art or one's psychic abilities, we deepen the connection with ourselves and foster feelings of well-being and completeness.

The third eye plays a large part in your ability to connect to and express your spiritual nature, vision, dreams for your life, and creative side. Being the doorway to the genius within, it receives inspiration, motivation, and creativity from the highest self. Your awareness of the third eye and its potential is what brings life to it and activates it, inviting your spiritual aspect into the wholeness equation that includes mind and body.

Five Ways to Allow Third Eye Chakra Healing

- Bring daily awareness to the third eye chakra. Your focused attention to the middle of your brow for just a few moments throughout the day can serve to not only remind you of your spiritual nature but also activate the third eye through the energy brought by awareness. It's an excellent way to reset your focus and allow clarity to be cultivated, as awareness is what brings things to life.
- Invoke the power of imagination. Our imagination is created by the third eye and is what we use to pull our desires and dreams from the unified field. Forming mental pictures and creating the feeling of the desire fulfilled is like flexing/exercising one's spiritual muscles. Like a muscle, the potential of the third eye needs to be activated and used to grow and build positive, forward momentum.
- Set a vision for your life. Begin by deciding what's possible for you based on your spiritual understanding and awareness of your oneness with the highest self rather than experience and human conditioning. Our humanness has its purpose and place, but not when it comes to dreaming big. Setting a vision so big that it inspires and gets you excited to get up every day will motivate you to take the inner and outer actions to bring your vision to life.

- Cultivate an awareness of your psychic abilities. They need your energy through awareness—your permission—to activate and come online. Everything is just a potential until awareness is brought to a particular thing. With awareness, potential becomes a possibility. Allowing your intuition to express through you as inner knowing and recognized energetic nudges will serve you greatly, as they will assist you in decision-making and navigating your life with greater clarity and confidence.
- Know that you're being divinely guided on your journey. We are never alone, nor are we without spiritual assistance. Your spirit guides, including your highest self, are ready and waiting for you to consciously connect with them so you can approach life more empowered through insight and understanding. Taking a few moments to go within and ask with an attitude of gratitude that your spirit guides and/or highest self reveal themselves as clarity, wisdom, synchronicities, and intuition will set a stage for connection.

Cultivating Intuition for Your Highest Timeline

Intuitive abilities are natural extensions of our inner being and serve the purpose of helping us reach our full potential. There are a few things to be mindful of if the desire is to allow them to be of assistance in aligning with your highest timeline. Given the opportunity through awareness and a willingness to be divinely guided by being present and alert, your intuition can serve you well in navigating life's challenges with greater perspective and ease. Cultivated intuition and its effects can arrive as feelings, spontaneous inner knowing, energetic nudges, synchronicities, and signs. The key to developing your intuition is the now moment, as the clarifying and ascending energies found within it raise your vibrational frequency, elevating your consciousness, which enables you to perceive the spiritual tools and insights being extended from spirit.

Let's look at some key points surrounding the development of your intuition. Each insight leads to the next, expanding your awareness in the process.

- Intuition is essentially your greatest power. From being able to discern divine guidance, assisting you in tapping into your creativity, helping with problem-solving and decision-making, your sixth sense connects you with the Divine and all its potential. Its immense value needs recognition because from that space of awareness and appreciation, it can be viewed as something quite deserving of your attention and nurturing.
- Your psychic abilities have a consciousness of their own. Just as we are expressions of Source with our own individual consciousness, so too, are our psychic abilities extensions of us. And just like us, they have a desire to express themselves, such as, but not limited to, clairvoyance (extrasensory perception), precognition (advanced knowledge), claircognizance (inner knowing), clairsentience (reading energy), and telepathy (mental communication).
- Don't try, but rather, allow for their expression. Our human conditioning can snag us here, as we've learned that effort or trying gets results. This is not the case with spirituality or spiritual expression. The elements required for the spontaneous expression of your intuition are mindful awareness of

them, your presence and alertness, and the desire and willingness to be guided. Know that you're always being divinely guided and learn to trust the messages being received by realizing that your psychic abilities are there to serve you.

- Intuition presents itself in subtle ways, but there are exceptions. I have found that for the most part, our psychic abilities arrive as gentle and often subtle feelings or as inner knowings. But I have also found on rare occasions that more obvious measures—intense feelings or energies or even the temporary manifestation of a spirit guide—are needed to grab my attention when it's imperative that I become aware of something about to happen. Remember that our psychic gifts are not limited, and they are nothing to be afraid of. They are spiritual abilities that require understanding.
- A focused mind makes intuition that much easier to perceive and act upon. The practice of being internally quiet offers you the clarity to be able to detect and receive information in the form of energy and inner knowing. In this receptive, empowering, and surrendered state, the offers of insight and intuition are easily recognized, appreciated, and utilized to assist one in manifesting their life consciously.

Clarity Exercise

When activated and open, the third eye affords you the spiritual perception to see life through the clarity of stillness or silence. A merging of your conscious mind with the mind of Source through surrender, you become the silent witness—who you are in spirit—as you recognize oneness. When reaction is experienced, it's recognized for what it is, and quickly and efficiently dissolved in the presence of your inner being—that's the transformative power found in unconditional love. With a picture painted of the clarity experienced through an open third eye, let's now turn our attention to the exercise, which is designed to guide you to align with the clarity of spirit (your soul).

A quiet space is preferable, but it's okay if there's some background noise during the exercise. Get comfortable, sitting is best, with shoulders relaxed.

Your eyes will be closed only initially as you take four or five deep breaths with your focus and attention being on the area in between and just above your eyebrows. With each breath taken, know that you're sending activating energy to the third eye. You may feel some tingling/opening in your forehead as you do so, and it's completely natural.

Once the initial deep breaths have been taken, open your eyes and begin to breathe normally. Drop your shoulders once more. Begin by bringing your awareness toward the space surrounding you—the nothingness. If thoughts arise during the process, let them; just be aware of them, resist nothing. If there is stillness (no thought), wonderful; just be aware of the inner silence. Continue to observe and be the inner presence to your outer world, focusing only on the nothingness surrounding you for two to three minutes.

Next, bring your awareness to the objects in your surroundings. See what's around you without attaching any labels; just be the silent witness to it. If there's a picture on the wall, look at it without any judgment. If you see a desk or a lamp, again, observe without definition. If thoughts are present, that's more than okay; continue to observe them through nonreaction as you look at the environment around you. Do this for two minutes.

For the last two minutes of the exercise, bring your awareness back to the nothingness, the space all around you. Recognize the formlessness surrounding you and allow it to reflect nothingness back to you. The inner reflected experience is one of silence—transcendence of the thinking mind when all labels and judgments are suspended. This results in clarity or clear seeing—recognizing the nothingness that is consciousness, that connects everything and everyone as you merge your conscious mind with formlessness.

To end the exercise, take a few deep breaths and let the moment go. It's best to approach this exercise without expectation, as it will allow for potential and possibility, including the spontaneous expression of the soul as clarity. It's key not to try to make something happen during this process but allow. You are free to practice this short, but effective exercise daily, and it should only take eight to ten minutes. The more comfortable you become inviting clarity and the oneness it offers, the greater the possibility for a spontaneous third eye activation.

Third Eye Chakra Affirmations

Potential is what the third eye is all about, as its activation unlocks dormant spiritual faculties that enable you to embody and express your full potential through self-actualization. The following affirmations are intended to activate and bring balance to the third eye as well as deepen your awareness of its ability as they are inspired from higher dimensions.

- I am connected to the clarity and wisdom of the third eye.
- I honor and trust my intuition.
- I choose to see myself and life through clarity.
- I am operating through an activated and open third eye.
- I recognize the spiritual within and without.
- I am always divinely inspired and guided.
- I see beyond the world of form and recognize oneness.
- I am connected to my inner knowing.
- I allow for the spontaneous expression of my psychic abilities.
- I see myself and others clearly through the present moment.
- I recognize my intuition in all its expressions.
- I am empowered to imagine and call forth my highest timeline.

NINE
Crown Chakra: *Become One*

This is the chakra of transcendence, where limitation ends and deep spiritual connection and embodiment begins. An activated third eye casts out the false self, leaving it orbiting one's consciousness. It's that process that dissolves the wall of separation between you and Source. What remains is the direct and continuous experience of oneness and inner peace. It's within this nonresistant state that you realize the spiritual and vastness of consciousness within and without. Because it represents formlessness, there really is no element that is associated with it.

Through the transcendent state you're fully aware that you've never left Source, nor has Source ever abandoned you. You've awakened to the kingdom within, including its spiritual treasures, and realize where you are, home in the spiritual realm. Because you're beyond limitations, things like psychic abilities, dormant spiritual faculties, mystical events, and even otherworldly encounters can come to life or be experienced because you're operating through universal or cosmic consciousness. Recognizing that unconditional love is all there really is, you know you're safe because you're empowered through the light and strength of oneness. You understand that you are unharmable because Source is your fortress and unconditionally supports, guides, and loves you.

Insights into your multidimensional self come to light as you tune in to the formlessness of spirit. Because of that, you may remember past lives, which are parallel lives taking place in the now moment when viewed beyond linear time, or experience déjà vu when visiting a place you've never been before. You realize that enlightenment is only the beginning and that there are no limits to consciousness or how many rooms (dimensions) there are to the mansion (the mind of Source).

By consciously becoming aware of your oneness, you are not only reminded of your creative power but are also enveloped by the energies of the unified field. This includes but is not limited to unconditional love, joy, bliss, happiness, clarity, wisdom, understanding, and support. This is what describes spiritual success and what confirms one's embodiment of the highest self, as well as one's potential reflected by an incredibly high vibrational frequency. It's what allows one to come into a new earth, the integration of the spiritual and physical.

Five Ways to Connect Deeper with the Crown Chakra

- Think, speak, and act from an awareness of being one with Source.
- Cultivate an understanding that there is an aspect of you that is transcendent of thought.
- Practice seeing oneness through mindful awareness.

- Remember that life is spiritual in nature—that the unified field is here and now.
- Embody your highest self by extending understanding and compassion to yourself and others.

Signs You're Activating and Opening the Crown Chakra

- You've had mystical or paranormal experiences.
- Oneness is being recognized more often, even spontaneously.
- You feel lighter and more spiritually connected.
- Spiritual gifts, such as psychic abilities, are expressing themselves more regularly.
- You're seeing the bigger picture and not sweating the small stuff anymore.

Shadow Work Prompts: Addressing Specific Crown Chakra Blocks

Ultimately, shadow work paves the way for a more resilient, integrated, and authentic self, leading to a more conscious and deeper connection with Source and others. This process fosters emotional regulation and intelligence, enabling us to live a life more aligned with our true values and potential. The following energetic blocks are meant to shine a spotlight on some of the main challenges we experience as humans. Because the issues are of a mental and energetic nature, they require a conscious and energetic approach. Let's begin:

Feeling Separate from Everything/Everyone

Lacking mind, body, and spirit awareness creates the idea of separation within and without. The belief in separation from Source is what disconnects us from directly experiencing stillness within, which clouds our perception of the spiritual world surrounding us. The following should also be mentioned because it needs to be addressed: being disconnected from the physical body causes uneasy thoughts, as it blankets our awareness to the fact that what we think, emote, and speak has an impact on our vibrational frequency, which is reflected in the physical.

Inner Work: Tuning in to oneness requires the conscious decision to let go of the thought of separation by recognizing that it's based on the limitations of human perception and relying solely on the five senses. Coming from this space of awareness, one can employ many ways to overcome the feeling of separation, such as practicing meditations and exercises geared toward recognizing oneness, connecting with others, expressing oneness affirmations, and remembering to be present. Employing these practices through intention sets the stage for experience sooner or later.

Being social and cultivating friendships can be fulfilling and bring about a feeling of unity. Nowadays there are many ways to connect with others, both in-person and virtually. Offline, you can meet and connect with others through volunteering, taking a class, or engaging in community activities. Online, you can make connections with others through social media, online forums, and communities that bring people together who have shared interests and values.

Our thoughts and words shift us into parallel realities—new and different experiences. Consciously affirming your oneness is what instantly on an energetic level shifts you into that experience. Remembering that what you affirm is done in the here and now further propels you forward and toward the desired outcome.

Being present allows you to really be in tune with the mind-body connection, allowing you to feel the energies within and surrounding you more fully. This deeper awareness can serve you greatly, enabling you to detect energies more clearly that are not in alignment with your wholeness. Awareness leads to transformation—a shift in energy toward the positive—because it involves the conscious mind, your awakened aspect.

Affirmations: "I am aware of my oneness with all of life," "My spiritual nature is based in oneness," and "I recognize I am already in the unified field."

Fear of Losing Control

The idea of surrendering to a higher power or stepping into an awareness beyond what we're used to can be a roadblock to ascending in consciousness, especially when one values their independence and autonomy. As human beings, our tendency is to try and control things, such as the process and outcomes. There's an inherent wanting to know what's going to happen next.

Inner Work: Understandably, control provides a sense of predictability, which to our human nature is comforting. But here's the thing: true change doesn't take place when we're in our comfort zone. There are a few things to consider that can offer clarity surrounding the fear of losing control. The act of surrendering to the highest self doesn't negate your will but empowers it through oneness. Aligning with the highest self enables you to consciously take control of your inner world of thought and emotion, which is key to manifesting a life of peace and fulfillment. Inner and outer resistance, at the level of crown chakra awareness, is viewed as futile and energy depleting.

One's independence and ability to make decisions are only enhanced through the insights and vision afforded through universal consciousness. No longer swayed by fear or external forces, one can more fully express themself through authenticity. An activated and open crown chakra allows for direct experience with the highest self, which is never controlling but allowing personified. Being the source of your inner guidance system, your inner being has the desire to be remembered so it can equip you with the divine wisdom and intelligence to live your full potential.

I have always found that profound change and even miracles can take place when one steps into the unknown. The reason being that all things become possible when we relinquish control and allow the spontaneity of the soul to express itself. The highest self knows what we require at all times, and when we get out of the way, we allow what's needed to arrive in divine timing, whether it's insight or wisdom to help with decision-making.

Uncertainty can be challenging, but life, by nature, comes with challenges. When we can make peace with this realization and accept it, challenges don't appear as such. With cultivated faith and trust, one can be certain that what they're intending for their life, their desires, are in fact coming to fruition—based in knowingness. The key is to become comfortable being in the unknown by consciously tending to fear because it's where a variety of potentials can come to life.

Affirmations: "I embrace my evolutionary journey and the change that comes with it," "I am a magnet for positive change in my life," and "I am comfortable stepping into the unknown."

No Sense of Self

Lacking a sense of self—who you are spiritually—makes it difficult to navigate life and also results in not knowing what you desire out of it. This state of being causes indecision, as one is unclear of their potential and what's possible. Entertaining this idea is what often makes one feel stuck and limited, which blankets one's awareness to the incredible potential and vastness of consciousness that is experienced through the crown chakra.

Inner Work: The crown chakra has nothing to do with playing small in terms of one's self-concept. Its purpose is to plant your awareness and focus on your oneness with Source. The high-vibrating cosmic energy of the crown chakra provides the ability to commune with Source on a continuous basis, clears all limiting or separating ideas, and highlights your spiritual identity. The experience of oneness doesn't require effort or struggle, but instead it needs the recognition of one's spiritual reality and the willingness and desire to remember one's spiritual origins.

Becoming one with the self ushers in clarity and spiritual insights, and it activates potentials that serve to remind you of who you are and what is possible. This transformative process sheds you of self-imposed limitations as you step into a life of greater meaning and purpose. This is not to discount the human experience but to highlight the fact that looks are deceiving. There is a spiritual heavy hitter within us all, and it's the soul.

Affirmations: "I know who I am in Source," "I am a limitless spiritual being," and "I am supported and divinely guided always."

Constant Boredom

A result of having forgotten that one already has the keys to the kingdom, including one's creative potential embodying a boredom state of being, is affirming one's lack of creativity. It also supports a feeling of being disconnected from a higher power. Boredom can also often stem from a lack of vision and motivation, which closes one off from the inspiring and renewing cosmic energies offered through the crown chakra.

Inner Work: The work involved here requires a break in routine in your thinking, beingness, and doingness. Entertaining old thoughts and limiting beliefs creates the feeling of boredom. Shifting your focus by recognizing your inner potential and cultivating an awareness that is fresh and new is only a decision away, and this can be just the spark you need to finding things to become excited about. Choosing different thoughts consciously, creating a vision for your life, and seeing opportunities within difficulty are ways to overcome boredom and disinterest.

New, empowering, and exciting thoughts can't be left to chance, nor can we wait for external change to happen before we experience them because that's a trap that would keep us waiting perpetually. Your conscious mind is the director, and its purpose is to choose that which you desire to experience. Tapping into your imagination reveals that there are no limits to what you can dream or to what is possible. This insight should not only excite you but also motivate you to embody the changed person now who is passionate and thrilled about manifesting positive change in their life.

One's elevated vibrational frequency, feelings of the desire fulfilled, and new outlook set the stage for change. These things empower you to take action to complete the manifestation process as you choose a direction for your life. Acknowledging your potential provides direction and confidence to look beyond where you are and see a different path. You can shift out of stagnation, limitation, and boredom by seeing things differently, trying new approaches, and realizing that failures are steps toward greatness and the realization of your dreams. The cultivation of perseverance backed by a vision for your life by knowing who you are spiritually will serve you well in living a life of passion, creativity, service, and fulfillment.

Affirmations: "I am excited about my potential and the possibilities that are in store for me," "I am a conscious cocreator with Source," and "This life is already taking off."

Overly Materially Focused

There is nothing wrong with enjoying the things that life offers. But when one is attached to external objects, finds happiness in possessing them, or is constantly seeking the next thing to bring them joy, it's this ever-seeking state of being that is a trap. It's also one of the ways we're prevented from realizing the immaterial—the spiritual.

Inner Work: You can be certain that what you're attached to has attached itself to you. Attachment is a type of energy—possessive energy—and because of its attaching nature, it clings to its host while also creating a fear of loss. It's very similar to gluttony, only in this case, we're talking about material objects, not food. Attachment energy is never satisfied and always seeks to add to itself to feel good. The key to breaking psychological attachment is to realize that your inner being is attached to nothing because it's one with everything.

Part of our human programming is to base happiness on externals, such as positive outcomes, people, or things. The trap in operating in this fashion is the disappointment and sense of loss that takes place when those things or people are no longer a part of our experience. Cultivating nonattached happiness by choosing it enables you to call it forth by simply thinking or expressing, "I am happy." To put it another way, spiritual happiness is knowing that you are one with Source, and that you are safe, divinely guided and unconditionally loved and supported no matter what. It's this inner knowing that creates elevated energies and feelings to spontaneously arise, further raising one's vibrational frequency.

Practicing nonattachment is vital in one's spiritual and healing journey, as it will alleviate much grief, disappointment, and sorrow, including the fear of loss. The interesting thing is that the more you practice nonattachment, the more receptive and magnetic your vibrational frequency becomes to attracting things because it tells the universe that "I'm happy no matter what." It's this egoless approach to life, relationships, and material objects that allows one to enjoy them without the worry of loss, which elevates you beyond the physical and consciously into the realm of spirit.

Affirmations: "I enjoy all that life offers without attachment," "I am connected to everything and everyone," and "I am one with the highest self."

Feeling Vulnerable to Life's Challenges

The accumulation of negative emotion over time can make many of us increasingly sensitive to adversity, making personal issues feel daunting and hard to overcome. Emotional pain weakens our ability to be resilient and has a negative impact on our nervous system, making it hyperactive due to an excess negative charge. It's one of the ways the body expresses what the mind has accumulated.

Inner Work: Strength and resiliency are two attributes of spirit that need to be examined and developed to shift from a vulnerable mindset to a more energetically healthy and relaxed state. Your soul is the expression of strength because it is indestructible, unyielding, and unwavering. It is resilient because it accumulates nothing through experiences—positive or negative—because it is nonattached. It would be accurate to describe the soul as being anointed, as nothing sticks to it.

The key is to approach life only one moment at a time, or breath by breath, as this is soul aligning. This more focused strategy to life allows you to deal with what's in front of you and not what could go wrong. This is renewing because it shifts attention inward and has a calming effect. The next thing to be aware of is that because we're made up of energy, we can shift states rather quickly by changing our perspective and deciding not to give our challenges so much weight. Going one step further, you can offer gratitude now, knowing that the answer or resolution to a problem or issue is on its way.

What should also be mentioned is that every moment is an opportunity to be reborn energetically. This can be tangibly experienced as a continuous feeling of relief when we bring this concept to life by resonating with it. What you say with knowing expands from the mind to the body, and expressing "I am reborn moment by moment" is what commands the subtle body to follow suit. Living more presently and with intention is how inner strength and resiliency to life's challenges are cultivated.

Utilizing a practice to release accumulated negative emotion, such as a mental exercise and developing a calm state of mind by choosing peaceful thoughts consistently, are excellent ways to prepare you for life's challenges. You can come to a point where they're seen as opportunities for growth rather than things to be afraid of or dread. Having the ability to see life, especially adversity through elevated points of view, reveals spiritual maturity, signaling your increased resonance with the crown chakra.

Affirmations: "I am strong and resilient," "I am more than capable of withstanding any challenge or adversity," and "I am renewed and strengthened in stillness."

Remembering Your Multidimensionality

The most important part of remembering your multidimensionality is the potential that is within it. Allow me to clarify. Your multidimensional self is based on the countless different frequencies and dimensions that it occupies all at once, in the here and now. The frequency you align with—whether it be anger or happiness, confusion or clarity—is what you become in the moment and is what's experienced as your current reality. Your multidimensional or highest self exists within all these frequencies regardless of what state of being you're embodying, as it encompasses all dimensions.

The great news about having this insight is knowing there's already within you a 5D enlightened version that personifies the clarity of stillness, the wisdom of 1,000 lifetimes, the understanding of Source, and a peace that is otherworldly. This enlightened self is the soul that is at the core of every version of yourself that you could embody. It is unchanging, unmoved, eternal, faithful, and invulnerable.

Your multidimensional self doesn't stop at the various versions of yourself that you can embody. There is another layer to your multidimensionality, and it includes past/future lives, which are parallel lives because everything, in every dimension, place, and time, is taking place in one instant—the now. Trying to wrap one's brain around this concept may seem futile, as I've come to understand it's transcendent of the thinking mind. One is either in a space of accepting or disregarding this insight. The point in offering this glimpse into our multidimensional reality is to shed light on how we already access, and can continue to access with greater understanding, the inspiration and abilities that seem to come from nowhere.

Our inner being is connected to the other lives we're living in this now moment. The soul is greater and vaster than one can begin to comprehend. There are three levels to our multidimensionality. There's the singular level, which is the life you're currently experiencing as a human being. As we elevate our point of view and have a broader picture, there's the next level, where we can see that the soul is experiencing multiple, even hundreds of lives all at once—in this dimension and in others. This has personally been confirmed by the countless UFO sightings I've had in my backyard that began in October 2020. I've posted hundreds of my encounters on social media and even had some of my more profound encounters featured on the Travel Channel's *Paranormal Caught on Camera* in 2024, season 7, episode 4. From the moment I had my first close encounter with a triangular object together with two neighbors, I experienced an instant remembering. Every encounter has been peaceful, uplifting, and even humorous at times. Through the direct experience of oneness, I've realized that nothing is truly alien; there is only that which has been forgotten or remembered. In interacting with these objects, the unified field or oneness has also been confirmed, as these crafts, although at times appear to be thousands of feet away, will often respond to my requests to power up, often just before I ask.

The third and most expanded level is through Source, which we share our oneness with. From this third level of awareness, we are one with everything and everyone in every place, this dimension and beyond. We are one with and are the rock, the tree, the car, an ex-girlfriend, an ex-husband, a former friend, the bully from elementary school, the teacher we admired, and the parent we resented on an energetic and mental level. This is why forgiveness and its application are so powerful and liberating.

When we hold anger, hate, or resentment toward another person, we're only holding it against ourselves because we are all one. Understanding this, we can consciously choose to extend forgiveness to our trespassers, freeing us from the past so we can move forward and upward in consciousness and life, enabling us to turn our attention and focus on what's really important—being our authentic selves.

Crown Chakra Healing Meditation

This meditation is essentially the most powerful and transformative practice you can use not only on your healing journey but also in coming into your full potential and highest timeline. It assists in replenishing your vital energy while expanding your awareness of inner stillness in the process. This meditative practice has the potential to spark a spontaneous third eye activation, the key to embodying universal or cosmic consciousness. Through a cultivated awareness of its importance and value in its ability to offer clarity, inner peace, healing, wisdom, and the experience of oneness, this meditation ultimately could be invited to one's experience daily.

You can introduce this meditation into your spiritual practice once or twice weekly, increasing it as you feel guided to. It only needs about ten minutes of your time as a starting point, from which you can progress, inviting stillness increasingly into your daily life as you feel called to.

Get into a comfortable position in a quiet area. Preferably, you're sitting up, your head is straight, and your shoulders are dropped as you relax into the moment.

Take a few deep breaths as you close your eyes and bring your attention inward. The power of our consciousness is such that what we look at with clarity (nonjudgment) dissolves. You are now going to bring your awareness to the thinking mind without judgment, just observation. As your attention is on the conditioned mind, slightly shift focus and become aware of any space, or "nothingness," between your thoughts.

Spend the next four or five minutes simply becoming aware of the space, the stillness between thoughts. This nothingness is your true essence—the presence or soul that is you. It is formlessness and without attachment, your 5D or enlightened self.

Next, take a deep breath and open your eyes as you continue being aware of the stillness within. Allow the nothingness of stillness to extend outwardly to your surroundings as nonjudgment. Spend the next three or four minutes silently observing both inner and outer environments. At this point, you may begin to experience oneness, including peace as inner silence—just allow the experience to blossom and expand. You may even feel waves of energy across your face and body; this is the subtle body being felt, and nothing to be alarmed about.

As you're meditating, remember to remain present-moment aware and relaxed by releasing tension, dropping your shoulders as needed. If you were unable to recognize stillness during the meditation, don't be frustrated; it's a process that will unfold in divine timing. The important thing about this practice is intention and the willingness to experience the peace and oneness of stillness.

To end the meditation, take a few deep breaths, bring your awareness back to the here and now, and let the moment go. Give thanks for stillness and for the unfolding of consciousness within you.

General Crown Chakra Healing

There is tremendous potential in terms of healing and untapped wisdom available to each and every one of us. Understanding this concept guides one's attention, creating an atmosphere for possible direct experience of one's spiritual gifts. The potentials and possibilities of the unified field start with awareness, as one's awareness is the activating factor; it's that which gives life to unseen potentials. Becoming familiar with the attributes of the highest self (which include strength, invulnerability, peace, and nonattachment), putting them into practice, and embodying them now is how to energize, activate, and heal the crown chakra—by being your whole self—in mind, body, and soul.

Exploring your connection to spirit provides life-bringing energy to the concept, which can potentially guide you to realizing cosmic or universal consciousness. Being open to divine guidance and having a willingness to step outside of routine patterns and embrace the unknown can lead to profound transformation. The highest self knows the most efficient path to getting you where you desire to be spiritually, if the goal is spiritual embodiment. It also knows how to confidently guide you through challenges and assist you in manifesting your desired life effortlessly, saving you time and aggravation. You have but to recognize and pay attention to the cues, wisdom, and divine guidance always being offered. It's cultivated alertness and discernment—aspects of being awakened to Source within—that allow the clear expression of information from the unified field to your conscious mind.

Five Ways to Allow Crown Chakra Healing

- Recognize and understand the strength of the soul through contemplation. The soul is eternal, unlimited, can accomplish anything, and is strength personified because of its oneness with Source. The soul doesn't tire, become exhausted, or moved by externals because of its very nature; it is the wellspring for limitless energy and the source of all vitality. Becoming aware of these attributes brings clarity regarding your spiritual nature and offers a glimpse into what embodying the highest self would be like—making potential a possibility.
- Your inner being is invulnerable—unharmable, in fact. What that means for you is that because it's powered by oneness, it is immune to negative thoughts and emotion.

Bringing your awareness inward toward the stillness of the soul will afford you the ability to transmute anything unlike unconditional love through conscious awareness. By embodying your spiritual nature, fear that was once the source of your suffering becomes a reminder to come back into alignment. You are invulnerable in essence, and by becoming aware of it and acknowledging it as a divine aspect of your inner being, you allow it to come to life.

- Inner peace is your natural state of being. Based in the understanding that formlessness represents your spiritual reality and that everything is an extension of your consciousness affords you the clarity not to be afraid of thought forms or negativity but instead see them for what they are. Inner peace is not just the absence of fear but the discernment to recognize it as it arises and the ability to dissolve it through the centeredness of your being by being in alignment with stillness. The highest self is unmoved by fear, and taking its lead is what shifts you into an empowered state where the tables are turned on fear.
- Making it a practice to see things from differing points of view makes us more open-minded and flexible in our thinking. There are as many shades of gray as there are humans on earth. Honoring other people's perspectives as their truth is a sign of elevated consciousness because it's one that doesn't need to impose its viewpoint on others.
- Invite the experience of oneness daily through mindfulness. Cultivating the awareness of oneness is probably the most powerful, transformative, and healing inner action you could take toward embodying the wholeness of your

being. Trusting the process, remembering that all of Source is for you, cultivating compassion, being of service, and approaching creativity through a mind, body, and soul approach are ways to tap into and remember the oneness of your inner being.

Becoming One for Your Highest Timeline

Oneness is an elevated awareness and the clarity that knows it's much more empowering, fulfilling, and expansive to integrate the larger part of oneself to their life. It's an awareness of inner balance that's reflected by each chakra being activated and opened through surrender by choosing nonresistance. Navigating daily life starts with vitality and energy as one jumps out of bed. You're aware that you call forth reality, so you begin with positive, life-affirming intentions at the beginning of your day, backed by gratitude. Stillness is at the forefront of one's consciousness and accompanies you throughout the day. This means that spiritual attributes, including psychic abilities, are invited and expressed, providing you with a greater sense of ease and confidence, even when challenges arise.

Relationships are cultivated through compassion, understanding, mutual respect, and the knowing that we are all one. Focus is placed on creativity, one's passions, and being of service. Scarcity and lack mindsets are left behind as one becomes aware of the extraordinary potential and abundance that's available within and without. Life is lived through a state of grace as one communes continuously with the highest self. You will still experience the conditioned mind, but it's now looked at with greater understanding rather than something to be feared.

Ways to Embody Oneness

Being heart-centered and internally focused and cultivating humility are powerful ways to deepen your connection to spirit, life, and others. Your heart space emanates unconditional love, which provides nonjudgment toward others. By lifting yourself higher into the heart chakra, you recognize the self-reflective nature of judgment. It's this heightened awareness that allows you to see yourself in everyone and everything.

Paying attention and directing your focus toward your inner being and listening to it deeply, past thought and emotion are revealing and unifying. This practice can lead to profound self-discovery and expansion of consciousness beyond the confines of one's human nature. Being open-minded and willing to grow and learn makes you receptive to wisdom and spiritual guidance. It's this humble approach that further connects you to the Divine as you nurture a sense of humility. Recognizing that all the gifts of spirit come from a higher power further inspires a lifelong desire for alignment and a deep reverence for the source of all truth.

How Oneness Translates to Your Highest Timeline

Your highest self reflects your highest potential. It does so because it's transcendent of limitation. Unlimited in every way, your inner being has the intuition and foresight to assist you in aligning with your highest timeline as you create a vision for your life. You're making decisions for yourself from a space of confident inner knowing.

Oneness Exercise

This short, simple, but effective exercise will serve you by having you realize your oneness with everything and everyone. You'll need a pad of paper and pen or an electronic device for this exercise. Preferably you're in a quiet space. This should only need about ten minutes of your time and needs only to be referred to as needed after that.

Get comfortable, drop your shoulders, and relax into the moment.

Take three to four minutes and reflect on the concept of oneness and how it translates into experience. For example, if we're all one, then that means all minds are joined through oneness and held together by the spiritual web of telepathy. Once you've spent some time reflecting, ask yourself the following question: When I've thought about someone or something, how often have I received a text or a call soon after from the person I was thinking about or encountered the thing I thought about? Write down your answer and then take a minute or two to reflect and see if any other insights or revelations come to mind.

I find this idea often really helps others understand oneness whenever I've done talks about interconnectedness: what we feel, project, or extend to another person or thing is what we instantly experience within ourselves. For example, let's say you're hammering a nail into a wall, miss the nail, and instead hit your thumb. The pain is intense, and the next thing you know, you're angry and cursing the hammer. Your anger and frustration are immediately felt and returned to you because it never really left you—you and the hammer are one. You can't get angry at anything without self-inflicting it first. The same thing happens with people. On the flip side, you can't experience appreciation and gratitude for a friend or a partner without extending it to them because the truth of the matter is that the appreciation and gratitude never left you because you are one with the other person.

Take the next three or four minutes and reflect on what's just been shared. If it resonates with you, great; if it doesn't quite yet, that's more than okay as well. The goal here is to offer clarity into the concept of oneness and allow you to come to your own understandings and conclusions. Once you're done reflecting, decide for yourself to move forward with the spiritual implications of oneness and how it can serve you by working with it through forgiveness, surrender, and creativity versus resisting it through identification with the conditioned mind and its projection of separation.

Crown Chakra Affirmations

These timeline-shifting affirmations are designed to help you connect to your spiritual nature and highest self on a deeper level by reminding you of your continuous connection to spirit. As you affirm the following statements, do so with an inner knowing and conviction as you remember your oneness with Source. These powerful acknowledgments will also serve you in having you feel a greater connection to life as well, assisting you in remembering your greater purpose.

- I recognize and embody my oneness with Source.
- I am aware of the interconnectedness of life.
- I am open to receive clarity, wisdom, and understanding, now and always.
- I am aware and align with the stillness within me.
- I am renewed and strengthened through stillness.
- I am connected to cosmic consciousness and its divine wisdom.
- I am at peace with myself, Source, and all of life.
- All is more than well, now and always.
- I am attached to nothing, as I am one with everything.
- I am an expression of unconditional love.
- I am one with the highest self and in alignment with my highest timeline.
- I know and recognize who I am in spirit.

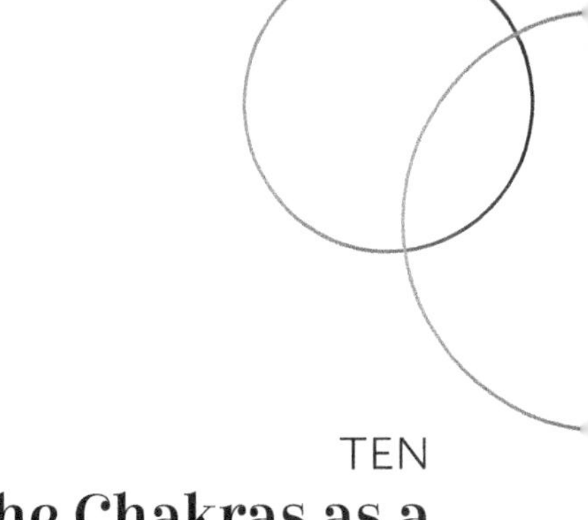

TEN
The Chakras as a Power System

By putting spiritual principles into practice, your awareness expands, unifying mind, body, and soul and enabling your chakras to spin freely through wholeness. The more you understand the chakras and the expressions of consciousness they represent, the less time you'll need to consciously let things go, as a high-vibrational frequency and their combined light automatically transmutes negativity. Your highest vibration reflects spiritual unification, where you move with the rhythm and current of creation.

Operating through wholeness awareness, every chakra is energized and opened by cosmic energy. You experience the stability of the root chakra, the ease of the sacral chakra, the power of the solar plexus chakra, the compassion of the heart chakra, the truth expressed by the throat chakra, the clarity of the third eye chakra, and the transcendence offered by the crown chakra. Being inwardly focused allows the divine intelligence within to deliver to you whatever is needed in the moment.

The thinking mind is still used to accomplish necessary daily tasks but it's no longer the dominating consciousness—you are free of its limitations and grip. The energies of wholeness are always ready to assist, guide, and remind you of who and what you are. This is not done through thought or emotion but by vibration, feeling, and knowing. It is subtle and gentle, but through focused attention the messages are clearly received.

As your three aspects work in unison, you bring wisdom, calm, and peace wherever you go. Going about your day, your high-vibrational field positively impacts whatever environment you're in, rather than you being impacted. Consuming lower energies in its presence, stillness is your shield and fortress, making you unharmable to negativity. This is done automatically, simply by being aware of who you are as you're alert and present. One has realized the infinite intelligence that's available to them, and so they choose to be divinely guided in all aspects of their life, knowing that all of life is for them.

Eighth Chakra: Cosmic/Soul Star

I waited until we were near the end of this book to introduce this cosmic energy center that is an extension of one's inner being and a potential within us all. The activation and coming online of what I prefer to refer as the cosmic chakra is a natural progression from embodying your spiritual nature. Located above the crown chakra and extending itself in every direction infinitely, this chakra enables you to tangibly and visibly experience other dimensions that include having encounters with what many describe as extraterrestrials but who are in fact facets of the multidimensional self. Bright white is associated with this chakra, as it represents transcendence, purity, and one's connection to the cosmos. I felt it important to introduce the reader to this chakra because Earth is going through a collective shift in consciousness and stepping into a higher dimension, which will allow more people to see what has always been present, just out of sight and mind.

Becoming aware of and understanding what this chakra represents creates the possibility of tuning in to its potential, which includes connecting with star family. Over the years, I have heard many stories, through documentaries, of people, including children, expressing the fact that they know that they're not from here but come from the stars. Some will refer to themselves as starseeds and express that they have an inner knowing that they're here to assist in the unfolding of a new earth and assist in humanity's ascension by anchoring in their powerful cosmic vibrational frequencies.

With many hearings recently taking place on UFO phenomena, and sightings being reported all over the world, governments are slowly trying their hand at disclosure, reporting what already is present in our skies. My goal here was to introduce the reader to this chakra and its potentials while offering some insights into this multidimensional potential and share that more people will be tuning in to it as humanity continues to ascend in consciousness. Our collective ascension and spiritual evolution will sooner or later reveal that we're not just human beings but also cosmic beings with connections beyond Earth.

Enhanced Intuition and Clarity

While psychic gifts such as telepathy and clairvoyance are always present to some degree, their full potential is realized when all chakras are activated and functioning optimally, leading to an extraordinary increase in intuitive abilities. There are some extraordinary effects of being superconscious, which is a state of mind beyond human awareness and perception. Some of the gifts that can be tapped into include the ability to see the world around you more clearly, to access profound insights to help others solve problems, and to get a deeper understanding so you can personally act upon the divine guidance.

With the subtle or light body activated, high-vibrational energy elevates your perception, allowing you to see and engage your world in a more meaningful and connected way. There's a sense of sacredness with daily interactions as you recognize the spiritual in others. With the chakras spontaneously expressing themselves through you, life is viewed with gratefulness, as you find happiness through the simple act of being. Life finally makes sense, and you bask in the knowing that you can make of life what you will. There's an understanding on a deep level that it responds to your intentions and vibrational frequency.

Throughout my years as a spiritual teacher and guide, I've had many people come to me looking for a way to get past a problem or find out their "whys." When you're deeply connected to your intuition, you can readily find answers to problems and help others move forward in their journey. As you acknowledge the divine power and intelligence that extend from the chakras, your conscious mind integrates with them. When developed, this inner connection opens a path for the receiving of insights and greater perspectives, which can lead to clarity and even facilitate another's healing process. Our activated intuition is incredibly revealing and confirms there's a spiritual aspect to us containing potentials that can transform our lives for the better.

With the third eye open, one is fully receptive to divine intelligence and guidance that, when acted upon, can elevate one's life on so many levels. Your highest self knows the way. It not only inspires your desires and dreams but also knows the most efficient path to realizing them. The keys are knowing you're being guided and being open to the information being given. As spiritual listening skills are practiced and refined, one arrives at a place of unwavering intuition, leading to a deep sense of self-trust and overall clarity of mind. You know you can trust in your life's divine plan and understand that nothing has been left out in terms of what you require; Source knows you that intimately. Being comforted and reassured by this inner knowing, you relax and allow goodness to flow through you and to you.

I should mention that being extraordinarily sensitive to energy has not in any way been overwhelming. Before my shift in consciousness, psychic events and insights left me feeling somewhat bewildered and unsure of what to do. I wasn't sure why I was picking up on insights and information from others. Little did I know that we do this all the time, but because we're distracted from what's really taking place, it's dismissed or not fully received. As spiritual beings, it's natural to automatically pick up on energy as information because all minds are joined. Our interconnectedness is what makes our intuition possible, allowing one to read energy like a book.

Boundless Energy

Mental exhaustion and burnout become things of the past when the chakras are working in unison. With less thinking and more beingness, energy is conserved through a quieted mind and a relaxed body. Time and energy are no longer spent focusing on things beyond your control, freeing up resources for conscious creation and action. Unrestricted access to universal energy offers several benefits, including an increase in vitality and stamina, improved mood, and an overall boost to motivation. With your energy centers in alignment, their unified power can accomplish extraordinary things, making anything seem possible.

When your mind and body gain access to the limitless reservoir of consciousness, the energy flowing through you infuses your cells with divine light. Because you're consciously plugged into the universe, you are reenergized on a moment-by-moment basis. This connection results in the feeling that you can handle anything that comes your way. There is a remarkable aliveness experienced that awakens your senses and inspires you to try new things. By embodying vitality and strength, you feel more capable than ever; where you once may have been just surviving, you're now glowing and thriving.

Our mood is often reflected in our energy levels, and being on the receiving end of high-vibrational energy can have one feeling lighter, uplifted, and more enthusiastic about life. The feeling of enthusiasm has a cascading effect in that it will boost your overall sense of well-being and satisfaction. It often leads to excitement about potentials and possibilities in your life, which causes even greater optimism. This positive momentum allows one to remain emotionally buoyant, even when the occasional emotional intensity is encountered. That's because the force and energy behind these feel-good feelings is nurturing and transformative; its main goal is to support you and assist you in accomplishing what you set out to do.

With being energy-abundant comes the motivation to engage in life on all three levels of being. Operating through a high-energy state is clarifying, which results in the ability to focus and process information better. It also leads to clear goal setting and direction, which encourages a proactive approach to mental and physical well-being. Our divine light not only energizes us but also speaks to us through inspired thoughts, ideas, and feelings. This motivates us to take mental and physical action to not only improve ourselves but also cultivate continuous energy levels.

When you're spiritually firing on all cylinders, unlimited energy resources become a very direct and tangible experience. Spiritual energy, by its nature, is expressive, and by receiving it fully we are renewed and transformed, allowing us to become positive agents for change in the world. This energy is already yours to harness and experience. It awaits your invitation and command to become active in your inner and outer life.

Discipline: A Foundation for Success

The chakras always follow our lead and support us in whatever we undertake. As we harness their potential, discipline allows us to be committed to realizing a goal through determination. A mind that is focused on achieving something will negate anything not in alignment with it, including a thought that's self-sabotaging, in its tracks. Procrastination often prevents us from progressing, and the key to overcoming it is to be mindful of the result if we stray from being committed daily.

Led by the solar plexus chakra and supported by the rest of the chakras, cultivating discipline daily keeps you on track and has a tremendous impact on realizing your goals and dreams. The concept of being disciplined needs to really be examined so it can be recognized for its incredible value. Being disciplined creates a determined mindset, allows you to have better time management, and supports short- and long-term goals. Discipline is the foundation for personal and professional success, a key ingredient in achieving self-mastery and peak performance.

The energies created by discipline remind us of what's important and where to focus our attention. This kind of focus allows us to effectively prioritize our day-to-day activities, saving us time and energy. Fostering consistent habits and routines helps us become more productive, developing leadership qualities in the process. Operating in this fashion, we are empowered to break down large projects or tasks into smaller, more manageable steps. This changes our perception of daunting tasks, making them seem quite doable.

Short- and long-term goals become achievable when we're consistently in alignment with them in mind, body, and soul. With all three of your aspects working together, success becomes an inevitability. Temporary setbacks are sometimes part of the process, but with consistent focus on the goal and action, your momentum continues to build toward the desired result. Our minds are incredibly powerful, and that power needs to be recognized and harnessed through determination to experience its full effect.

The power of discipline supports the journey of personal growth, which can be translated into the work and services one provides, enhancing the overall experience. Discipline, as an energy, seeks to see things done to completion with competence. A potential within you, when activated and developed, can lead you to greatness in all aspects of your life.

How to Quantum Leap

There are a few key elements that, when realized and put into practice, can result in massive upward and forward shifts in consciousness, catapulting you forward months or even years along your spiritual journey. In the context of personal growth and achievement, quantum leaping refers to making remarkable and accelerated advancement in a short amount of time. It can be a sudden breakthrough from a long-held trauma or a sudden change in your trajectory leading to a change in circumstances.

Through inner and outer action, these elements can shift you suddenly toward healing and growth and also in alignment with your highest timeline. These elements include changing your personal story, realizing that your desired future is already created, focusing on its reality through visualization, and embodying the person now who is already living that dream. Understanding just how powerful and transformative these concepts are is the first step in realizing their potential to not only assist you to make inner shifts but outer ones as well.

Many of the stories we tell ourselves are based on, especially when it comes to achievement, things that didn't work out or have gone wrong. It's important to note that perception plays a large role in rewriting our life story, and it must begin by realizing that nothing has gone wrong. An unrealized dream or goal was based on a version of you that was operating from a mindset that may not have been in full alignment with the intention, as so many of us have. A failed relationship or business doesn't have to be labeled as such but instead can be viewed as steps toward growth and success. You can change your mind and personal story now by no longer referring to what hasn't happened and instead stating what can happen, as this signals the chakras to prepare to support you. Affirming the following on a consistent basis and powering the affirmation with action changes your present trajectory upward and forward: "Everything is always working out for me now and always. I am focused on positive change and embody it. My conscious thoughts, words, and actions are causing me to leap forward in life."

Before we imagine the dream and set the intention, Source has already answered and the desire is fulfilled on a vibrational level in the unseen. Know that you're not having to create anything but instead must come into alignment with it in mind, body, and soul. Your full potential is unleashed when all aspects of you agree and are in harmony with the desire. Your full excitement prepares you to receive as the universe mirrors that energy with the manifestation of the fulfilled wish. Being decisive, you clear a path that in effect is more direct than meandering, saving time.

We're all quite aware what happens when we focus and repeatedly give our energy toward undesired scenarios and images in our minds. The effect is we lower our vibrational frequency and feel hindered in our progression. I bring this up because the opposite is also true. Taking a few minutes throughout the day and envisioning and feeling the desire as fulfilled now shifts you into energetic alignment with it. Doing so is also a reminder and is motivating to continue to take the forward, seemingly small steps to bring the ideal to fruition. Be mindful as you're imagining that you're not creating but aligning and allowing through feelings of appreciation and gratitude.

Ask yourself, "What would the version of me who is living their dream now think, feel, and act?" Reflecting on this question opens you up to the answer and serves as a guide for you to cultivate being that successful person now. I know from my own experience that this person is excited about their life, grateful for the experiences that led me to choose differently, and living through intention daily. Begin embodying inner and outer success and you'll unleash supporting forces such as inspiration and divine guidance to assist you in actualizing it.

Seeing the great value and forward-shifting potential of these key elements can assist you to quantum leap and make massive, positive shifts in your life. As you work with and embody these concepts, you'll continue to evolve, grow, and realize greater potentials within you. It all comes down to awareness and putting things into practice as you remember the power of your harnessed energy, which can advance you toward the life of your dreams.

Embracing Limitlessness

The state of oneness that is beyond any mental boundaries is a way to define limitlessness. In this state, the focus is toward the potential and creativity of the mind, the soul, and one's elevated vibrational frequency. With the chakras working as one, you unlock your full potential as the same unlimited energy that gives life to the universe expresses freely through you. Fulfillment is found by communing with the highest self and through your creative endeavors.

Operating through a limitless mindset allows universal forces to work in harmony with you, supporting your desires and dreams through greater insight and receptivity to divine intelligence. There are no limits to the kind of assistance that's available when self-limitation has been transcended. The universe meets us where we meet ourselves. It reflects what we are energetically and provides what we're ready to receive.

Limitlessness as an energy and consciousness doesn't look at the physical body; instead, it only recognizes the unlimited nature of formlessness: stillness. As humans, the tendency is to identify with thoughts and form, believing we are the bodies we inhabit. It's this perspective that convinces us that there's difficulty in overcoming obstacles in our lives. Your higher consciousness is transcendent of the physical body, form, and the manifested world altogether, as it recognizes the unlimited potential that's available in the unified field.

A limitless mindset reflects the conscious awareness of the highest self and understanding that there are no limits, as none have ever been placed upon you. To tap into one's latent potentials, one must recognize *the Limitless within*—stillness—and allow it to express itself through the combined power of the chakras. The following three insights will further assist you in understanding and embodying an infinitely expanded awareness and mindset.

Limitlessness Insights

- Your inner being is limitless, a wellspring of untapped potential and a source of infinite creativity and wisdom. An attribute of spirit, potential doesn't need to be added to you, but instead recognized and activated through thoughts, words, and deeds. The more you reflect on the concept of being limitless, the more you will invite and align with the life-changing energies that reflect it.
- Limitlessness is based in unity consciousness or oneness. Recognizing one's interconnectedness changes the way you see yourself. Through reflection, you become aware that you are an essential part of the whole, which gives your life greater meaning. When it comes to self-realization, you're only limited by your imagination. This empowering mindset affords you the ability to look and feel beyond the five senses, as infinite intelligence guides you through inspiration.

- A limitless mindset thinks, speaks, and acts through the awareness that every part of oneself is creative. With inner knowing, one affirms: "I am limitless. I can accomplish anything. If I can imagine it, it already exists vibrationally." A shift from looking to the outer world for confirmation on what's possible, one looks to the highest self and its unlimited creative power and potential.

Empowered Manifesting

There has been a lot of information written on the law of attraction and manifesting since the mid-2000s. The focus is often on setting a vision, positive thinking, gratitude, feeling the desire fulfilled, and the power of belief. Those are all great concepts and part of the manifesting process. A few key concepts have been missing that, if put into practice, would empower one in becoming more effective at manifesting their desires. Inspired by the chakras, these insights will enable you to manifest with less resistance and greater confidence. The first concept is foundational, and it involves awakening to and embodying your highest self, which has been thoroughly covered in this book. The second concept deals with how to manage the doubt and mental roadblocks that inevitably creep in when one starts setting intentions. And lastly, the idea of consistent desire—aligning action to complete the mind, body, soul approach—is an important topic to discuss.

Manifesting from a wholeness awareness takes the process to an entirely new level. The focus is primarily on your conscious relationship with Source, and it's from that place of power that you manifest. Being complete and fulfilled from within first, you're able to feel ease about the process and enjoy the journey, rather than wait to feel more fulfilled when the desire manifests. This approach also allows you to manifest through inner knowing, which is more powerful than belief, as it activates your will fully. With your chakras guiding and inspiring you, you become clear on your preferences, with the knowing that your desires and dreams are inspired and fully supported by the universe.

Being able to shift out of doubt and worry during the manifestation process becomes effortless when you're keenly aware of the enormous power of your elevated vibrational frequency. Knowing that your primary function is to tend to limiting thoughts and emotions, you consciously transmute them, as they're based in fear not facts. To put it bluntly, fear is a liar. There, I said it, and it needed to be said. What I mean by calling fear a liar is that relative to your spiritual nature's ability to observe the inner/outer worlds without labels because fear deceives, only painting with darkness. With this knowledge, you can have an empowered attitude toward negativity. In knowing how to neutralize it, you can prevent it from sabotaging your dreams. Embodying such a self-empowered state of being creates a tremendous amount of powerful, forward momentum. The momentum builds to such an extent that, when lies are presented by the false self, you will be able to sit back and laugh at them, knowing they cannot prevent you from achieving your goals.

We're going to round off this section by discussing the importance of completing the manifesting process. My observation is that many of us have fallen into the trap of believing that one only needs to set the intentions, elevate their mood, and then patiently wait for the desire to manifest. Although an elevated vibrational frequency that is receptive does in fact work in some instances, to achieve uncommon results, one is going to have to take action because that's what completes the process. You can think and feel abundance but without being of service in some way, without giving, one cannot fully receive. Extraordinary health and healing can be thought about, but if one is consistently eating in an unbalanced way or engaging in unhealthy habits, the intention cannot be fully realized. Consistent, aligned action, even small daily steps, takes what the soul inspires and what the mind focuses on and makes it a possibility and ultimately a reality in divine timing.

My hope in having offered these important pieces of the manifesting puzzle is to clear up any confusion or frustration. You have the potential to manifest the life of your dreams through chakra activation and soul awareness. Every experience or manifestation begins with a thought, a potential that exists within us. The energy that follows on the levels of mind, body, and soul determines the outcome.

ELEVEN

Shifting into Higher Timelines Consciously

Recognizing and acknowledging the fact that you already possess all that you require to embody and shift into higher timelines sets the stage for their expression. That's true abundance! It's based on your conscious connection to the universe, which lays the foundation for an abundance mindset. Within us are miracles ready to transform our life experience, including spiritual faculties such as our imagination and the reality-shifting potential of the chakras. These potentials only need to be remembered and applied to remind you of the inner abundance you have at your disposal.

There is so much potential and possibility that comes through this expanded awareness that applies intention and directed focus in the process. I need to highlight a few key points that will assist in reminding you of what happens when you recognize and use what's already been given to you. Here are eight insights into the effects caused by operating from an abundance mindset:

Abundance Mindset Insights

- You're able to change your emotional state at will through intention, knowing you're always working with energy and that it responds to your direction. Being cognizant that attention, awareness, and focus give life to experience, you focus on the positive. Internal abundance is recognizing the fact that states of being such as bliss, joy, and fulfillment are potentials that can be called forth and embodied through choice. It's knowing you don't have to rely on external conditions to change to feel happiness or uplifted.
- Having an abundance mindset offers relief from fear and a scarcity mindset. It empowers you to radiate elevated positive energy, which acts like a magnet. It can attract abundance in the form of a desired partner or like-minded people, such as those who are a part of your soul tribe. It can draw unexpected opportunities into your life, which can translate to greater fulfillment personally or professionally. Your ability to call forth such experiences stems from understanding the power of nonattachment and surrender, which opens you to Source's fulfillment of your deepest desires.
- Your self-confidence and trust in your capabilities are enhanced with an abundant state of mind. With access to the clarity and wisdom that reside within, and by listening to the divine guidance always available, doubts are laid aside. You know you're spiritually equipped to rise to any occasion. This developed self-confidence and trust in yourself is based in fearlessness that allows one's inner being to be remembered. This inner being is confidence personified and knows what it's capable of.

- When you're spiritually connected, miracles are not exceptions but the norm. In fact, every moment is recognized as a miracle through an abundance mindset. Being natural expressions of spirit, miracles are spontaneous in nature. Synchronicities abound and are readily recognized as messages or opportunities to act upon. Things seem to fall into your lap, and it's a result of focusing on prosperity and providence. This state of mind also creates the possibility of miracles being experienced as a spontaneous awakening and even physical healing.
- You live more fully and experience greater richness through an integration of spiritual consciousness. Everything feels more alive as you merge spiritual awareness into your daily life. Bringing the presence of your inner being to every encounter, casual conversations become sacred moments as the sacred is recognized within and without. Dullness and boredom essentially vanish as the joy, bliss, and liveliness of spirit is integrated into daily life.
- Your highest self is now your sole measure of who you are and what you can become. Transcending limited perceptions allows new potentials, new possibilities, and a new earth to unfold before your eyes. Knowing that your vibrational frequency is what's important in being able to shift realities, you tend to your inner world. You know that life will sooner or later reflect the positive shifts that have taken place within you.
- Your overall well-being is profoundly enhanced through the embodiment of stillness, as it's at the heart of the treasure chest of abundance you have. Every spiritual gift, psychic

ability, tool, and faculty is found within and is expressed through stillness. Being in communion with stillness enables personal transformation and one's evolution continuously. This enables you to maintain incredibly high energy levels provided through the energies of oneness.

- An abundant state of mind gives you the green light to manifest your dreams and desires. By having cultivated faith and trust, which are large parts of an abundance mindset, you're able to think big and engage your imagination, visualizing and feeling the desire fulfilled. With expanded awareness and inner knowing, one also understands to let go of how and when the desire will come to fruition. Trusting in divine timing, you enjoy the process of sifting and fine-tuning that which you desire as you let go of attachment to outcomes.

All these potentials and more are available and tangible through an abundance mindset. Recognizing that there are no limits to consciousness, potentials and dreams become possible as life is given to them through awareness. While belief is important, truly knowing the power of your mind to shape reality is even more powerful; it's the key to unlocking your inner abundance.

Maintaining and Raising Vibrational Frequency

The importance of maintaining elevated states of being is often overlooked in the hustle and bustle of everyday life. One's inner state of being also reflects a person's health on an energetic level, their experiences in relationships, and their ability to shift into higher timelines. Maintaining your vibrational frequency creates positive momentum, allowing other high-vibrating energies to express, which raises your field further. Energetic maintenance also cultivates resiliency, allowing you to rise quickly in consciousness even when you temporarily veer off track. We're going to look at some ways to maintain and raise your vibrational frequency that will serve as reminders, helping you understand that operating from expanded states of awareness is not as difficult to maintain as some may think.

Consciously choosing states of being such as happiness allows you to further raise your vibrational field when caused and expressed through spiritual awareness. The decision to use affirmations based in nonattachment, for the sheer desire to feel great and not as an effect because of what one has or attained materially, cultivates the ability to call forth higher states. By embodying the very energy one is focusing upon, such as joy, by simply affirming, "I am joyful" cultivates your ability to shift energetic states more efficiently.

Remember that negative states are part of being human and serve as catalysts for growth when their purpose is understood. Ignoring or suppressing negative emotion only delays the inevitable confrontation and hinders personal growth. Embracing them, feeling them, while not holding on to them, allows us to become more self-aware and evolve in the process. Used properly, negative emotions become our springboard into higher states of consciousness.

Check in with the body throughout the day, as it's your best gauge for determining if you're experiencing tension or stress. Doing a quick thirty-second scan from head to toe can be revealing and show you what needs attention and adjustment. We often carry tension in our jaws, neck, and shoulders. By taking a few moments to consciously reposition ourselves by relaxing our jaws, rotating our necks, or dropping our shoulders, we can disrupt tension. Becoming aware of where there's a concentration of tension/energy is often enough to dissolve it by sending healing/loving thoughts to the area. Affirmations backed by feeling such as "I am relaxed and releasing any tension within me" or "my energy is moving unrestricted" can assist in energy blocks and bring back balance. The practice of mind-body awareness can further deepen your understanding and therefore your ability to pick up on emotional imbalances, allowing you to consciously release them.

Eating a mostly balanced diet through consistent conscious decisions to fuel the physical body rather than feed the emotion of gluttony will serve you greatly in feeling good. The subtle body's purpose is to maintain energetic health and balance, and it serves as a nutritional guide when we tune in to its wisdom. When ignored, the subtle body will send messages and cues in the form of feelings and symptoms, telling you that your diet isn't in alignment with wholeness.

Focusing on gratitude and appreciating who you are in spirit brings feeling great to a whole other level. Delighting in your oneness with the universe cultivates deep gratitude. It also invites more timelines where you find yourself continuing to be thankful for who you are spiritually and for the blessings that come by embodying your spiritual nature. This heightened state of gratitude serves as a powerful magnet, inviting higher-vibrational energies as thoughts and feelings.

Being of service to others allows for soul expression that cultivates joy and fulfillment. As spiritual beings with a purpose, we are called to share and give of ourselves, whether it be our time volunteering or sharing our gifts or talents. It's through acts of service, regardless how small they may seem, that we invite the experience of fulfillment in our daily lives.

Consistently living from the inside-out rather than outside-in is self-empowering, as it maintains one's peace. Being inner focused gives us an elevated point of view that sees things more clearly and with greater discernment. Cultivating self-awareness and understanding surrounding both our human and our spiritual natures allows us to have options in how we approach and manage things in our life. It allows us to see things from different perspectives.

Spending time with cherished friends and family is nourishing to the soul, as uplifting energies are allowed to spontaneously express as joy, happiness, and laughter. Knowing that we have people that we can share our lives with—the ups and downs—hug, and just be ourselves around, makes us feel connected and loved. In being mindful of the fleeting nature of this experience we call life, we are reminded to be thankful for our loved ones, creating a deeper appreciation toward them, which is elevating.

Making inner peace is a priority because it's a powerful source of strength and fundamental for spiritual growth and embodiment. Often overlooked because of the demands of daily life and how subtle it is as an experience, inner peace requires us to recognize the importance of its cultivation. Anytime we're choosing to observe the inner world of thought, practice going with the flow, and integrate mindfulness into our moments, we are choosing inner peace. The key is recognizing how these practices align with our inner being and the peace it always emanates. This awareness, in turn, makes the embodiment of inner peace a richer and more tangible experience through stillness. It also strengthens us preemptively, enabling us to transmute anxious thoughts and feelings with greater efficiency through expanded awareness and the higher vibrations that come with it.

Remembering that life is spiritual in nature shifts your awareness from thinking things are concrete to being malleable to your intentions and desires. This mindset shift is not only freeing but also allows for you to hone your skills at working with and manipulating universal energy. Earth is where we remember how to harness our minds through direction so we can shift toward more desirable timelines. Understanding that one is the cause of their effects reminds them that they have the power to raise their vibrational frequency, maintain it, and also manifest their destiny.

Clarifying Your Preferences

As you evolve, grow, and come to understand more fully your potential to align with your desires, you may find yourself imagining bigger dreams for your life. Remember that when you're manifesting, you're not hoping or wishing for something to come to pass but calling forth what's already existing in the unseen realm surrounding us. You're not creating anything but coming into alignment with the desire fulfilled.

Thinking big reflects your conscious connection to the highest self, which inspires you. Most people begin consciously manifesting their desires from a more general framework. Affirmations at the early stages of manifesting may look like this: "I am abundant and prosperous," "I am attracting a loving and caring partner," and "I'm already working at my dream job." These are great places to start from, but by focusing in on and clarifying your preferences, you not only direct your energies more effectively but also reap the benefits that come with homing in on specifics. We're going to look at six benefits of clarifying your preferences as you manifest your desires.

Greater Inspired and Aligned Actions: Having clarity on what you prefer to have, be, or do will inspire you to take the focused actions necessary to come into alignment with the desire. The initial inspiration sets the stage, but the beingness and doingness that follow determine the outcome. Having clear preferences also helps you stay motivated, as you have a vision of the end goal to refer to and align with.

Focused Imagination Allows You to Embody the Desired Fulfilled: Seeing the specifics of your intentions in your mind's eye allows you to incorporate your physical and spiritual senses, feeling the reality of the dream now. This approach shifts your full awareness toward the desire, which recognizes its fulfillment.

Being Specific Saves You Time and Energy: This point is especially geared toward attracting the right partner. If you have an idea in your mind of what the ideal partner embodies and looks like, it not only gives you the inner direction and reminder to also embody those qualities but also saves you time, energy, and even grief by remaining focused rather than being distracted by potential partners who you know aren't a vibrational match.

Ability to Recognize Opportunities: Knowing what you desire and having a clear picture of what it is you wish to experience will provide you with the discernment to recognize when something is presented to you that will move you closer to its realization. Being clear is also an attractive and magnetic energy to embody, as it draws in potentials and synchronicities that resonate with your preferences.

Dream-Fulfilling Creativity: Your clear preferences will create the ideas, potential avenues to take, and ways in which you can share your gifts and be of service to others. Being in a purposeful space of awareness in terms of what you desire to express and experience summons like energies to support and see your wish fulfilled.

Know Where You're Headed: The power in knowing allows you to transcend emotions that would attempt to derail you. It directs your energy and keeps you pointed in the right direction toward the desired outcome. It confidently supports your will to impress your preferences on the universe, direct universal forces, and create a positive outlook.

The Power of Nonattachment

Having talked about clarifying your preferences, I felt it was quite important to highlight the power in being nonattached to outcomes, which includes how and when the desire will be fulfilled. Just as awareness is a superpower, so is nonattachment. Applying the practice not just to the manifesting process but also to everyday life is incredibly empowering, as it allows you to maintain inner harmony. Nonattachment is based on one's awareness of their inner being, who is transcendent of all attachments because it's one with everything and everyone. It's the ability and awareness to relinquish the need to control others or outcomes, as it's based in trust and faith.

We're going to look at how the power of nonattachment can be used in the various facets of your life and how it promotes well-being and, in the process, keeps you in alignment with your highest timeline. In this section, we look at one's overall well-being, relationships, finances, and health.

Overall Well-Being

Applying nonattachment in your daily life lessens your susceptibility of being energetically drained from the lows that are experienced in life. Not everything will go exactly as we plan or wish for, and learning to be at peace with life through a spirit of nonattachment allows you to transcend potential suffering. Developing an inner state of well-being that is nonreliant on the outside world maintains one's vibrational frequency. Operating in this sovereign-minded fashion, you're in alignment with the highest self and experience the harmony, steadiness, and balance of spirit, which empowers you to be resilient even in the face of adversity.

Relationships

Nonattachment in the context of relationships is an important topic that needs to be discussed. Approaching your partner, family, or friends with nonattachment removes the pressure from others of having to be a certain way. It creates harmonious environments and allows a person to transcend lessons that would be called upon to wake the person up from being attached and wanting others to behave a certain way. When one is operating from a space that needs others to be a particular way to make themself feel happy, one is bound to be disappointed, as others have their own free will. Nonattachment not only allows you to express yourself without fear but frees you from the possessive energies associated with attachment.

Finances

Money can understandably be a delicate subject to talk about in terms of nonattachment, but with some clarity, one can understand the futility and fear that's created when we base our peace, security, and happiness on what we do or don't have. Tying our state of being to money is disempowering because money is a form of currency—energy—and our relationship with money is within our minds. Having negative beliefs surrounding money or focusing on lack or scarcity, are in fact attachments in the form of fear—the fear of lack. Cultivating an abundance mindset based on your potential and not externals, developing trust in the process, and being grateful and appreciative for what you have now, shifts you out of a lack mindset and its attachments, liberating you from the fear of lack and loss.

Health

When we operate from an awareness that's forgotten the mind-body connection, that disconnection creates unconscious/negative thinking and emotions, as we are unaware that cause and effect operates through every facet of our lives, including health. Fear seeks to disrupt virtually every part of our existence, including the innate harmony of the physical body. These limiting ideas and fears are attachments that cause more fear because one's vibrational frequency is lowered in the process. Becoming aware of the mind-body connection and how thoughts and emotions have an impact on our well-being and health empowers us to apply nonattachment in this case, which will dissolve attachments, creating space for new and life-affirming thoughts and ideas that serve us in achieving greater health.

Be of Service

One of the fastest ways to realizing your dreams is to be of service to others by sharing your gifts, talents, and knowledge. The wonderful thing about combining action with the vision for your life is that it allows you to embody your desires in mind, body, and soul. The energy created through this wholeness approach is incredibly powerful and timeline shifting. Remember that whatever it is you have to offer to others is only a potential until it has been activated through action.

Being of service allows you to further cultivate a sense of purpose and well-being, creates a sense of fulfillment, gives insights into others' lives thereby giving you greater perspective, and develops a sense of community. What also results from the giving of yourself to others is a richer life experience that will create more opportunities for even greater acts of selflessness and kindness. You can't help but become more empathetic, more compassionate, as well as more grateful in the process, for who you are and what you're able to share to enrich the lives of others.

We are all called to be of service in one form or another, and it's our job to pick up on the inspiration, see the potential in how it can help others, and take the necessary steps to make it come to fruition. Reconnecting with your inner being is your soul purpose, and it's in that process of remembering who you are spiritually that your potentials and hidden talents are revealed. It is also the way in which you could be of assistance to your local community and beyond. When you're choosing to be of service, there is no limit to how large of an audience you can reach because of the power of interconnectedness.

Synchronicity Awareness

An expanded awareness of your spiritual nature and the spiritual realm that surrounds the manifested world opens you up to recognizing and receiving the signs, messages, and countless ways that the highest self and your spirit guides use to get their message across. Synchronicity from a spiritual vantage point is regarded as a miracle, a message sent in divine timing reminding you that you are acknowledged, supported, and guided. Understanding that synchronicity is always at play invites more and more divine messages and signs to manifest, as you're being cheered on by the spiritual realm.

In this section we're going to look at the positive results that can happen when you become aware of the synchronicities in your life that are intended to remind you to keep moving forward, stay motivated, and guide you toward realizing your dreams. By bringing awareness to these insights, you'll become more cognizant of not only the potential in synchronicity awareness but also the nature of miracles in the process. The closer you shift toward your inner being and the clarity it emanates, the more you'll realize and understand that every moment is a miracle unfolding as consciousness, the Divine expressing itself.

Enhanced Intuition through Expanded Awareness

Your inner guidance system, or intuition, is further enhanced as you allow for awareness to bring to life initial spiritual concepts and ideas. Reflecting on the concept of synchronicity invites your awareness, opening the door to experiencing spiritual communication and direction from the other side.

A Greater Sense of Oneness

Becoming aware of synchronicities and their divine timing further confirms your interconnectedness within the universe and those within it who are in support of you. Separation is nonexistent in the spiritual realm, and those who are your spirit guides, including the highest self, love you unconditionally and only want to see you succeed.

Deeper Insights into the Hidden Mechanics of Life

Synchronicity is based in unity, which extends into telepathy and one's ability to read energy. This includes the discernment to pay attention to one's environment and the changes in energy that take place during a synchronistic event. Communication and information extended from spirit has a particular frequency, one that is high vibrating and inspiring.

More Openness to Think Outside the Box

Experiencing synchronicity is expanding on many levels and allows one to go beyond the five senses as they tap into the sixth sense. Realizing that one's intuition is always online and operating is a reminder that there's a part of you that's transcendent of the physical body and its limitations. This expanded self-concept opens the door to greater insights and inspiration, which can lead you to finding solutions to problems or come up with a never-thought-of service or product.

A Greater Understanding into Consciousness, Miracles, and Spiritual Communication

The space within and surrounding you isn't empty because it's consciousness (Source) and it's teeming with potential, miracles, healing, and information in the form of insights and deeper understandings. This is confirmed when we're given a flash of insight, or a timely and much-needed message of hope or inspiration, to motivate us to carry on. There is potential in everything, including synchronicity because it all originates from Source. Synchronicity, like wisdom, moves in one direction, expressed from one's highest self or spirit guides to the conscious mind.

It's About the Journey

It can be easy to forget the unfolding process that is one's life, including the here and now, when one's sights are set on shifting into a higher timeline or focused on manifesting a desire. This is an important topic to discuss because it serves as a reminder that everything that one could truly desire in terms of the soul's attributes is available right now. Your inner being is a moment-by-moment experience, as is Source.

The balance that would greatly serve you would be to think, express, and embody the person who is experiencing their highest timeline now, or the desire fulfilled. Embodying your inner being through authenticity is key in this process. The soul has all the insight and intuition required to help navigate you along your journey.

By enjoying the process and living your fullest expression of who you are spiritually now, you will find that in fact it is about the journey, as life realized for what it is—spiritual in nature—will unfold in unimaginable and magical ways. For many, the snare is that they get caught up in waiting: waiting for their manifestation to arrive or waiting for the ideal partner, but the issue with that is one is embodying a "waiting" energy. Because of that, they will continue to wait. Embodying your inner being allows for the flow of cosmic energy, and operating through a mind, body, and soul approach creates the atmosphere for the spontaneous expression of miracles.

Understandably, there's a part of us that wants to know how and when things will happen. But if we can let go and practice trusting the process and divine timing, we can relax and become comfortable with the unknown, which allows potentials and possibilities to express themselves in the forms of timeline shifts and desires coming to pass without delay. What it all boils down to is realizing what really matters: who you are and what you're being right now. The spiritual journey is one of maturing, growing, and evolving. In making our relationship with Source a priority, one will find that whatever else manifests will simply be icing on the cake.

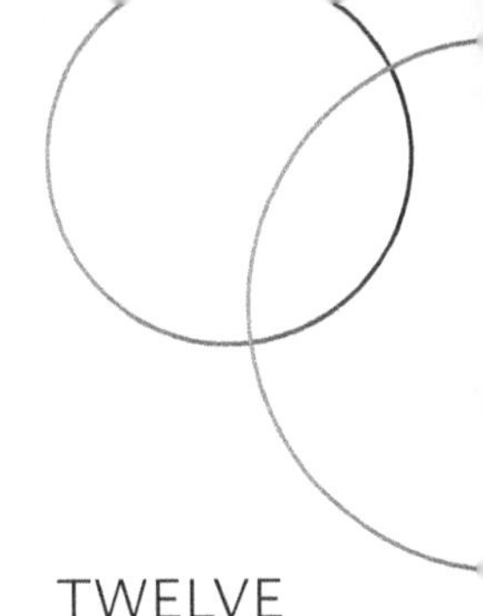

TWELVE
Spiritual Embodiment and Your Highest Timeline

The power of priority is vital when it comes to infusing excellence into all that you are and do as well as being the key to living masterfully. What we deem important dictates how we spend our time and energy. The things we value most shape our decisions and, ultimately, our outcomes. Making personal development our top priority is the most important investment we can make because it reflects the value one recognizes in their own life. We are a continuous work in progress and by choosing to challenge ourselves, adapt, and dream bigger, we summon the potentials required to continuously live spiritually successful lives and achieve extraordinary results.

It all starts with you, and my focus in this section is to light a fire within. I want to remind you that your level of intensity, specifically a white-hot desire, for personal growth and change is what gets the universe's attention. Making clarity, wisdom, and understanding your priority sets the stage for their eventual expression through you as your full potential unleashed.

As ever-evolving beings, we often require challenges to spur our spiritual growth and rise to the next level of awareness. Challenges cause us to seek solutions that open us up to new ideas and concepts that can lead to the uncovering of hidden talents and abilities. Approached consciously, we grow when we're put to the test, becoming more confident as our skills and character become more refined. As we become more aware of our potential and what we're truly capable of, we broaden our horizons and look forward to new opportunities.

Having a spirit of adaptability is an invaluable personal trait, as it allows you to thrive in today's rapidly changing world and enables you to be an effective problem solver. I often refer to a famous quote by Bruce Lee: "Empty your mind. Be formless. Shapeless. Like water. You put water in a cup, it becomes the cup. You put water in a bottle, it becomes the bottle. You put it in a teapot, it becomes the teapot. Now, water can flow, or it can crash. Be water, my friend." This powerful quote reminds us of the importance of adaptability—to be nonresistant—as to maintain the flow of universal energy and its transformative potential to shift and elevate us. When we are like water, we're able to flow and move with greater ease, allowing us to move forward, rather than remain stuck.

Dreaming bigger for ourselves is an act of personal expansion and a commitment to tapping into and embodying higher aspects of ourselves. It requires courage to dream big and step into the unknown. What helped me get over the idea of letting go of what seemed familiar and certain in terms of making a living, was the realization that what I was doing as a full-time healthcare professional could never manifest the life I was being inspired to live. Having tapped into the infinite potential of stillness, I become aware of what could be—how I could be of service in a more fulfilling way—which made the decision to follow my life's purpose and dreams that much easier. When I decided to get on board with my inner guidance system—my soul's plan for my life—I allowed untapped potentials and abilities to come to life that assisted me and propelled me forward personally and professionally.

Every human being is called to live their full potential, and it begins with making one's life a priority—in all its facets. Doing the inner work and tending to the self is not selfish—it's our soul purpose—it's the process of becoming egoless. It's by evolving and ascending that we return to being our authentic, unconditioned selves and remember our innate potential and power to shape our destiny.

Energetic Death Leads to Positive Change

There's a lot of misunderstanding when it comes to death. My goal here is to offer a perspective from the vantage point of someone who has experienced ego death and applies the concept of death as a mode for continuous change and spiritual embodiment. Death is transformation. Whether we're talking about someone leaving their physical body or letting a negative emotion die through mindfulness, death leads to change. In either case, the results are rebirth, expansion of consciousness, and spiritual alignment. This section will examine how a conscious understanding of death can be a powerful tool for continuously embodying the soul and having a deeper understanding of life.

The soul is always emanating the highest vibrational frequency, and it serves as your compass and gauge for alignment. It never falters and is a continuous beacon of light because it *is* the light. Your conscious mind is naturally drawn to this light and is the very thing that spiritual seekers are in search of. My point is to reveal that whenever you apply mindfulness to negativity, you're experiencing a mini death of ego and that's taking powerful, conscious inner action. Knowing this both heightens your awareness and transforms your perception of what seems to be just daily spiritual practice or shadow work. It does, in fact, have extraordinary effects on your ability to manifest your destiny and rise to the level of the soul, the state of enlightenment.

The practice of letting judgment, fear, and limiting self-concepts die is what allows for your continuous reawakening to spirit. The highest self represents transformation and ascension, and this approach takes its lead from it. Knowing what this approach accomplishes further deepens your understanding of personal transformation and what it means to be the soul through conscious, active self-work. Spiritual embodiment, in its truest sense, involves negating the false self and recognizing and aligning with the highest self. In a practical sense, it's integrating one's lower and higher consciousness. Overall, the human experience is enhanced by using what's needed in terms of memory and emotion while leaving limitation and what no longer serves you behind.

The highest self plays many roles, and the two main roles it plays in your embodiment of spirit is communicator of divine wisdom and understanding and a reminder to wake up. As the concept of ego death is understood and integrated in your spiritual practice, you'll become clearer regarding who you are. And in that process, your ability to dial into what's being divinely communicated to you will become more seamless. The highest self reminds us that every moment is an opportunity to awaken. A breath-by-breath practice is the key to continuous growth and change.

Highest Timeline: Oneness Consciousness

Oneness consciousness is far-reaching, and because of that, it enables you to extend the potentials within it through all aspects of your life. Your inner and outer experiences are transformed by the unifying energies of the unified field, elevating and enhancing all that you do. Never overpowering, the awareness, clarity, and energies experienced through stillness are for the most part in the background, coming forward when one expresses their higher truths.

What needs to be shared and underlined here is that your highest timeline is not off in some distant future but is a parallel reality available now, which becomes obvious when you cultivate awareness beyond the conditioned mind. The direct experience of oneness is a very here-and-now one, as oneness is the true nature of reality in this world and beyond. It's unchangeable and steadfast in its nature because it's what Source is. Source is the reason *oneness is.*

The foundation for coming into your highest timeline—unity consciousness with its healing, ascending, and supporting energies—divinely guides and inspires you to realize your fullest potential in mind, body, and soul. It accomplishes this by extending spiritual insights and guidance through a clear mind. The following are some of the profound effects of tuning in to and embodying oneness consciousness that enables you to expand beyond 3D consciousness and maintain elevated states.

Emotional Mastery

Cultivating your awareness from separation consciousness (the conditioned mind) to the elevated state of oneness consciousness allows you to create space and see the thinking mind from the eyes of Spirit. This clear vision speaks to you in vibration and understanding, which enables you to shift and become one with the silent witness: your inner being. No longer attached to thought forms, you become, through consistent practice, a master of emotion, as emotional intelligence is cultivated through expanded awareness.

Enhanced Discernment

Through quiet, focused attention, discernment is enhanced to supernatural levels. The clear mind that's experienced through oneness highlights anything unlike unconditional love, enabling you to recognize, address, and transmute negativity in the moment as it presents itself. Enhanced discernment doesn't stop at your inner world. It extends outwardly and allows you the clarity to read energy, others, and any environment you're in. Afforded through an activated and open third eye, spiritual discernment pierces the veil, sees potentials and possibilities, and empowers you in your decision-making.

Belief to Knowing

One of the powerful shifts that come through spiritual embodiment is that limiting beliefs are laid aside and replaced by empowering thoughts that are created from the highest self. Centeredness immerses your conscious mind with the mind of Source, which is knowing personified. This shift is what affords conscious, forward-moving thoughts as well as divine guidance to assist you in day-to-day life, enriching and empowering your life in countless ways.

Purpose and Direction

Direct spiritual experience confirms your soul purpose while also revealing to you the ways in which you can share your gifts, talents, and knowledge as you step into being of service to others from the soul level. You become a catalyst for positive change as you continue to explore what it means to integrate your divine aspects with your humanity. Doing the inner work creates ripples of beautiful and transformative energy that extend far beyond what you can imagine.

These are just some of the extraordinary results and experiences of realizing oneness consciousness. Understand that there are countless potentials, possibilities, and spiritual faculties one can tune in to through this expanded state of awareness. One's life truly transforms into a living expression of interconnectedness and becomes a canvas for boundless creativity.

Highest Timeline: Extraordinary Health

Your inner being is transcendent of the physical body. What that means for you is that by reconnecting your conscious mind to it, you raise your vibrational frequency to the point where only pure awareness remains. This allows cosmic energies to renew and strengthen you in mind and body. Worry and fear override the innate intelligence of the subtle body through identification with the thinking mind. This is part of the process as we take on a physical form, but it doesn't have to remain that way. You can shift inward and upward through spiritual awareness, which propels you into higher states of being and the extraordinary health they reflect.

We often hear of the mind-body connection, which describes the interconnectedness of one's mind and physical body that are unified through the subtle body. Just as our chakras are listening and respond to us, so too do our cells, organs, and systems because they are all expressions of consciousness. Understanding this, one realizes the value in cultivating and maintaining an elevated vibrational frequency because higher states of consciousness reflect inner peace, harmony, strength, and oneness, which are translated into the physical as renewal, increased energy, and vitality.

Knowing that our inner world, including our physical body, responds and reflects our state of mind, we can take conscious steps to cultivate extraordinary health. The most powerful inner action one can take to not only allow healing cosmic energy to fill our cells but also create the possibility of a spontaneous awakening is to become aware of and embody stillness. The direct experience of stillness unites mind, body, and soul, and what that reflects is wholeness. Through wholeness, cosmic energy moves freely, ushering in healing, while also automatically uplifting us.

The healing potential and power of stillness, from my experience, has no limits in what it can accomplish. Backed by the power of unconditional love, it is fully capable of restoring us mentally, physically, and spiritually. Extraordinary health is a state of mind and requires conscious inner and outer action caused by expanded awareness to be tangibly experienced. Inner action includes a deep awareness of the mind-body-soul connection, which affords you the insight to resolve negative energies within your vibrational frequency. Outer action includes conscious and balanced eating, and moving the physical body on a regular basis to maintain muscle mass and strength, have increased energy levels, and increase one's overall well-being.

Extraordinary health, or as I like to describe it 5D health, reflects a harmonious balance of mental, physical, and spiritual well-being. A state of vibrant and boundless energy with a deep sense of peace, one could say it's supernatural. Health is viewed as being an energetic state that can be improved by raising and maintaining one's vibrational frequency. It's an expanded state of being that recognizes dis-eased or uneasy/anxious thoughts and chooses instead to focus on wholeness and the life- and health-affirming thoughts and healing energies it expresses.

Highest Timeline: Harmonious Relationships

Integrating your awareness with the highest self heals your relationships with yourself, with Source. Deeply understanding one's human conditioning, having the ability to see others clearly, together with cultivated empathy and compassion are reflected in your relationships as harmony, peace, and stability. A conscious relationship with the self and others allows many other attributes to be reflected from one's expanded awareness.

We're going to look at five more positive expressions that come as a result of being in harmony with oneself and others. These attributes extend from an awakened soul and make for conscious relationships that highlight the deeper understanding and connection that are afforded by being mindful of the self.

Understanding and Empathy

When we recognize and understand our human limitations and the suffering that comes with them, we can take a step back and not take things so personally. Everyone is dealing with their own challenges and adversities, and not everyone is operating at the same level of awareness, which is a gift in contrast. From this point of view, one can choose to extend understanding and empathy through cultivated awareness and insight.

Clear and Honest Communication

The interesting thing that takes place when one realizes their oneness with Source and the strength and invulnerability that come with that relationship, is that one becomes unafraid to show vulnerability. This frees you of any shame or guilt in sharing your story and struggles, and how you overcame them, which can serve as a source of inspiration to others. Authenticity allows you to be clear and direct in your communication, which is often appreciated by others.

Appreciation and Respect

Your embodiment of higher states of consciousness allows for spontaneous soul expressions, such as joy and bliss, which create feelings of appreciation and respect toward oneself and others. Approaching relationships with the same kindness and unconditional love (nonjudgment) you give yourself allows it to be extended to others. We are all connected and joined through telepathy, and others can very often pick up on the vibes we are giving off. Being appreciative and respectful is what opens the door for receiving it back from others.

Nonjudgment

This is in essence the greatest gift you can extend to another person. The ability to see someone through the clarity of the present moment, even after knowing them for several years, elevates one's relationships, as one views them through the eyes of Source—through nonjudgment. The ability to extend this gift is healing and transformative to both the giver and the receiver. It also provides the concept of everyone being responsible for their own happiness, which ushers in great relief because we've all been conditioned to place our happiness in the hands of others and have felt the disappointment when their actions seem to fall short.

Extension of Forgiveness

Cultivating the maturity to be able to forgive and release oneself gives you the strength to extend it to others. This doesn't mean you have to reconnect with those who have trespassed against you, but the extension of forgiveness releases you of the anger and resentment accumulated from the initial wrongdoing. For those you wish to continue to share your life with, forgiveness extended with a spirit of forgetfulness—in other words, letting it all go—ushers healing into relationships and can even elevate them through continued personal growth.

Highest Timeline: Recognizing and Allowing Abundance

The key to allowing greater abundance to come into your experience in all its forms is to recognize the already present abundance one has within and without. Through the cultivation of awareness and deepening of one's spiritual nature, one finds the greatest treasure of all—stillness—and all the gifts and spiritual faculties necessary to empower you to live a spiritually successful life. It's by recognizing and acknowledging the vastness of consciousness within you, *that is you*, that you can overcome the limiting beliefs and thoughts of lack that prevent you from realizing the abundance in your life and the potentials for even greater expressions of plenitude.

A wholeness mindset highlights the fact that one lacks nothing in terms of clarity, wisdom, understanding, intuition, and the ability to consciously manifest their life, which are all gifts and potentials freely given from Spirit. Being whole also enables you to be grateful for what you have, knowing that there's more that can be accessed by embodying the fulfilled desire now. If you're experiencing a circumstance that no longer resonates the abundance mindset you've developed, remember that you are empowered to choose differently rather than focus on what is. Clarity reminds us that repeating a circumstance in one's mind with frustration and anger only further cements the experience in one's life, preventing one from advancing within and without.

The inner being within you seeks to express itself in all its potential abundance, which includes its ability to experience it as creativity, well-being, health, strength, energy, connection, joy, peace, and much more. Your authentic self knows no lack nor does it focus on what is, but what's possible. Knowing there are no limits to what it can accomplish, the soul thinks big because it is infinite potential. A shift from our learned limitedness, the soul causes your dreams and desires because it knows they can come to fruition. If it can be imagined, then it already exists in one form or another in the unified field.

Your task is to recognize the soul that you are and the life-changing potentials available to you. Intention together with the cultivation of faith, trust, and surrender will serve you greatly. It will shift you into a timeline that reflects your expanded and abundant vibrational frequency. Abundance is a state of mind, just as lack is. The very fact that we can choose lack in this world of relativity confirms that we can also choose otherwise. Abundance, like all the other attributes of Spirit, must be embodied, not just reflected on.

Embodying Your Highest Timeline

The ability to embody your highest timeline rests in your awareness that it already exists as a potential within you. You must simply remember that you can accomplish anything when you combine purpose and perseverance. You are the cause of your reflecting timelines, and you have the potential and ability to shift into desirable ones through the power of decision. Your highest timeline starts and ends with you. Nothing outside of you and no one else can prevent you from expressing it because it's solely an inside job.

What also needs to be emphasized is that your beginnings are not indicative of what you can become, have, or do. A clean slate is reflected by a new and different choice or perspective. What I want to impart and clarify is that our power of decision can reshape our lives in more profound ways than we can fully comprehend.

Every human being is endowed with the same potential to make their dreams a reality. The key ingredients are energy and the unwavering commitment to channel that energy into consistent thoughts, words, and actions. Success on all fronts must be chosen as the only option. There is a delicate balance of combining the drive to go where you've never been before with the faith to take the little steps forward that culminate your grandest vision.

Living through wholeness awareness transforms your life and lays the foundation to manifest the life of your dreams. Mind, body, and soul working consciously as one is the secret to elevating the human experience to spiritual heights. One lives masterfully by allowing every aspect of oneself to work in harmony with each other, beyond inner resistance and conflict, resulting in an incredibly fulfilling and rewarding life inside and out.

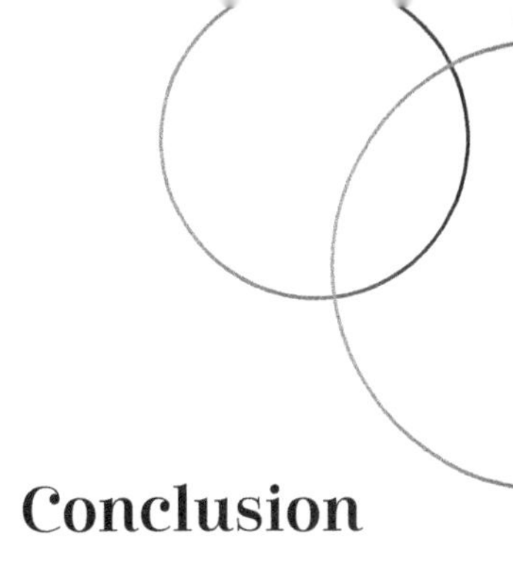

Conclusion

What I'm about to share serves as a gentle reminder: You must decide for yourself on a conscious level that life is for you. When identifying with the fears and the limitations, we operate contrary to the oneness that is life. Operating this way, we experience a narrowed perspective that creates inner conflict, resistance, and suffering. Our unconsciousness summons the wake-up calls to shake us from our slumber of the thinking mind and awaken us to oneness, to create a balance between form (thoughts) and formlessness (stillness).

Moving forward, simply remember that nothing is being done to you but for you. Life is set up to give you all that you desire—good or bad, wanted or unwanted—based on your vibrational frequency. Source doesn't judge our decisions; there are only reflections of the state of being one is embodying. You are free to shift and choose again; choose differently by recognizing the reality-shifting power you already possess. Operating from the idea that all of life is for you shifts you into a reality where that can be tangibly experienced on every level: mind, body, and soul.

I want to close this book by reminding you that effort and struggle are not necessary to access your potential and shift into higher timelines, but they do prevent you from realizing them.

You're already shifting into countless parallel versions of yourself as you navigate daily life through the different thoughts, emotions, and decisions you make. The key is to become aware of this fact and choose to shift consciously into a more preferred state of being consistently by understanding the futility in hanging on to and identifying with limitation. It all comes down to what's still serving you.

Just know that all things are possible and within you is already an ascended and enlightened being (your soul) who has two main desires: to know itself while with the physical body and to be able to express itself as clarity, wisdom, understanding, strength, invulnerability, intuition, and every other attribute it emanates. May you come to know and deeply understand who you are in Source, and may that be expressed for you as your full potential and highest timeline.

Many blessings,
Jiulio

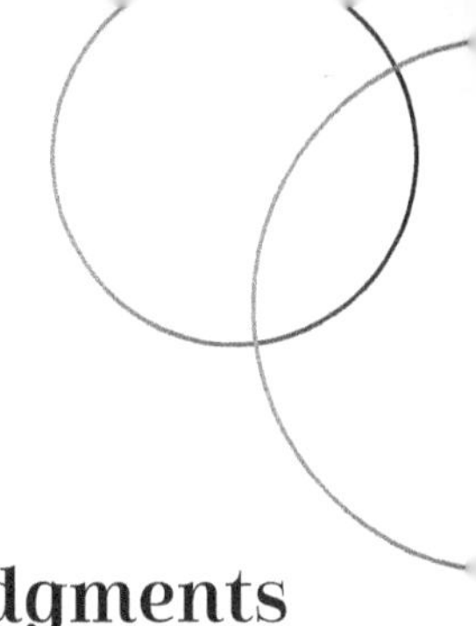

Acknowledgments

There are many wonderful and extraordinary people who helped bring this book to life, and I want to thank them. A big thank you to my editor, Amy Glaser, whose guidance and expertise are always welcomed and deeply appreciated. Thank you so much, Amy, for your vision and support. To my production editor, Stephanie Finne, I am so grateful for your meticulous work and guidance on this project. Your expertise and attention to detail have been essential in allowing me to bring my creative vision to life. Thank you very much, Stephanie. My sincere thanks to the cover design team for capturing the essence of this book so beautifully. And to the entire staff and team at Llewellyn Worldwide, many thanks for all that you do.